substance

KENGO KUMA

substance

7 INTRODUCTION
THE SUBSTANCE OF HUMANITY

WOOD

12 DOMINO 3.0
18 THE CLOUD
22 YURE
28 CIDORI
34 NEOWA DOME
40 KOMOREBI
48 BOTANICAL PAVILION
54 KODAMA
62 CASA WABI COOP
70 CLT PARK HARUMI
78 WOODEN HAZE
82 URO-CO
88 SANA MANE SAZAE SAUNA
98 NAKAHASHI
108 KUSUGIBASHI

BAMBOO

118 NANGCHANG-NANGCHANG
122 SENSING SPACES
128 BAMBOO PASSAGE
134 BAMBOO FLOW

METAL

142 ONE HEALTH CARBON GATE
148 OWAN
152 CASA BATLLÓ STAIRS
164 EPHEMERAL TENT
174 KUGI-KUMO
180 MUSHIZUKA
186 WAKUNI SHOTEN

CONTENTS

PAPER

194 PAPER SNAKE

200 IRORI & PAPER COCOON

TEXTILE

210 CERAMIC YIN YANG

216 CASA UMBRELLA

226 NAMAKO

236 KXK (KRUG X KUMA = ∞)

240 KITHUL-AMI

STONE

248 STONE FOREST

254 CAVE OF LIGHT AND SHADOW

APPENDIX

262 INDEX OF PROJECTS

263 BIOGRAPHY

264 AWARDS AND RECOGNITION

266 EXHIBITIONS

269 MONOGRAPHS AND PUBLICATIONS

INTRODUCTION

THE SUBSTANCE OF HUMANITY

KENGO KUMA

The foremost problem with modernist architecture is that it disconnected people from the substance of nature. In the same way that humans are composed of elements, so too is the earth, and consequently the materials used in traditional architecture.

However, modernist architecture attempted to avoid and ignore nature and defined architecture as being made from a structure (typically steel or concrete) and an outer skin (often glass or metal).

This definition was valid as a criticism of the stylistic architecture at the time, in which decoration was oversized and consisted mainly of an outer skin. As a result of modernism, the existence of the most significant substances–living organisms of people and nature–were viewed as unimportant and lost in oblivion in the rough dichotomy of structure versus façade. Before long, this resulted in a lack of substance in architecture, with it being suspended in midair and being between something abstract and cosmetic, hollowing it out physically and metaphorically.

In traditional Japanese architecture, this issue of being suspended midair did not arise. The separation of the structure and the skin did not exist in traditional Japanese wooden buildings. Wooden pillars were beautifully polished and served a leading role without any cosmetic decoration. They were both the structure and the façade. But before this, they were living organisms in nature.

The space between the pillars was partitioned with mud walls and paper screens and sliding doors (called *shoji* and *fusuma*). These served a structural role, providing the strength to resist earthquakes. The translucent *shoji* and flimsy-looking *fusuma* and balustrade absorb force during earthquakes, enabling buildings to withstand these seismic events without any supplemental components. All elements that comprise traditional Japanese architecture serve as the structure and the outer skin, and began life as natural substances. The modernist dichotomy never existed in the first place.

I was inspired by Japanese architecture to transcend this dichotomy. That challenge, or practice, is integrated into the collection of work in this monograph. All the projects are small, or relatively small for their typology. This scale enables us to try our various substances and materials, and to test different ideas. Opportunities for this experimentation and practice were provided by events such as the Venice Biennale and Milan Triennial, and at other times by academic institutions, such as universities and laboratories.

From a certain perspective, these opportunities can be thought of as 'social space.' Actual construction projects are controlled by the dichotomy of the structure and the outer skin, and the substance can only be handled as the outer skin and as a cosmetic element. However, between these different projects, we have some freedom. We repeatedly perform experiments in this 'social space.'

Various substances are used in these experiments. In addition to natural materials, such as wood, bamboo, paper, and stone, investigations with a wide range of other materials, including textiles, have been explored. We have taken on the challenge of various types of substances based on the notion that expanding the scope will expand the breadth of possibilities in the future.

AI and other cutting-edge digital technology is serving a major role in these experiments. In addition to structural computation, advanced information technology is involved in various processes, from material production to assembly, and this helps us a lot.

Before the digital age, humans processed substances and manufactured materials, which took the life from them. However, with AI and information technology we can now give life back to them, and people can live with architecture in which life has been restored. By experimenting with these substances and materials, we are repairing the relationship between people, architecture, and nature. This will lead to a greater sense of humanity as people and nature coexist together again.

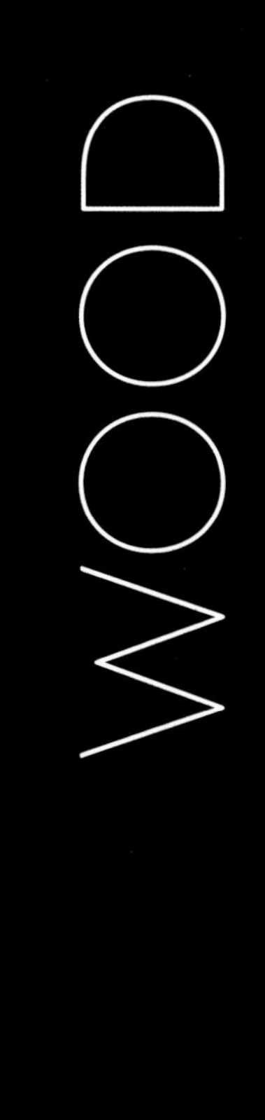
WOOD

DOMINO 3.0

LOCATION Venice, Italy **COMPLETION** 2025
COLLABORATORS Ejiri Structural Engineers
AI Professor Yutaka Matsuo (University of Tokyo)
STRUCTURE Professor Norihiro Ejiri (Japan Women's University)
TYPOLOGY Cultural, Exhibition
PHOTOGRAPHY Nils Koenning

The 19th International Architecture Exhibition at the Venice Biennale had the overarching theme of AI. We presented Domino 3.0: A House to Return to the Forest, which explored the dialogue and interaction between nature and advanced technology.

We used timber from trees uprooted and devastated by Storm Vaia, which affected northern Italy in October 2018. These salvaged logs had been left to decay on the forest floor. Each tree was scanned three dimensionally to record its unique features. The trees were then assembled with the assistance of AI to integrate seamlessly with each other while maintaining structural integrity.

The digital analysis enabled the design of 3D-printed custom joints that were embedded into and between the branches. These soft, flexible joints—responsive to movement and freely transformable—allowed the trees to be gently interconnected, forming a living, adaptive structure.

Domino 3.0 questioned contemporary architecture and society: By using actual trees, it proposed that cutting-edge technology does not exist to keep humans away from nature. Rather, it can enable humans to return to nature.

THE CLOUD

LOCATION Kraków, Poland **COMPLETION** 2021
COLLABORATORS Faculty of Architecture and Fine Arts, Andrzej Frycz Modrzewski Krakow University
TYPOLOGY Cultural, Exhibition **PHOTOGRAPHY** Kamil Krajewski

The Cloud is inspired by Polish and Japanese traditions of wooden architecture. Both cultures use angles to interlock timber components, thereby creating fixed connections.

The installation is an individual interpretation of traditional carpentry connections with slanted locks and dovetail joints. It is composed of two groups of long and short timber elements. They are connected with 45-degree diagonal locks, forming a complex and abstract spatial arrangement.

Modeled and generated using parametric software, the pavilion showcases the intersection between traditional carpentry techniques and advanced computer design technology.

The Cloud was displayed at the Manggha Museum of Japanese Art and Technology in Kraków in an exhibition titled *Kengo Kuma: Experiment. Material. Architecture.* It was produced by a local carpenter and assembled by students participating in the Polish-Japanese research and workshop program carried out in 2020 and 2021 by Kengo Kuma & Associates and the Faculty of Architecture and Fine Arts at Andrzej Frycz Modrzewski Krakow University.

YURE

LOCATION Paris, France **COMPLETION** 2019
AREA 376 ft² (35 m²) **TYPOLOGY** Cultural, Exhibition
PHOTOGRAPHY Antoine Barelhe; Stefan Tuchila

Yure is a wooden pavilion installed in Jardin des Tuileries for the Paris Internationale 2019 art fair. Part of Galerie Philippe Gravier's *Small Nomad House* series, the structure needed to be small, easily assembled, sustainable, and capture our underlying spirit of innovation.

The pavilion is made with identical wood pieces that are connected vertically and obliquely with traditionally crafted joints. The structure's appearance changes depending on the perspective from which it is viewed, shifting from open and transparent to closed and dense.

The space within the structure is divided into small areas over three separate floors; each accessed via a ladder, allowing free movement through and up the structure. Two teepee-shaped fabric tents can be draped internally, creating a secluded bedroom and lounge space. At the top is a viewing platform, like a terrace.

The name Yure translates to 'slowly moving in the wind.' It's light, dynamic, and evokes a sense of movement, in contrast to much of Paris's solid, heavy, stone buildings.

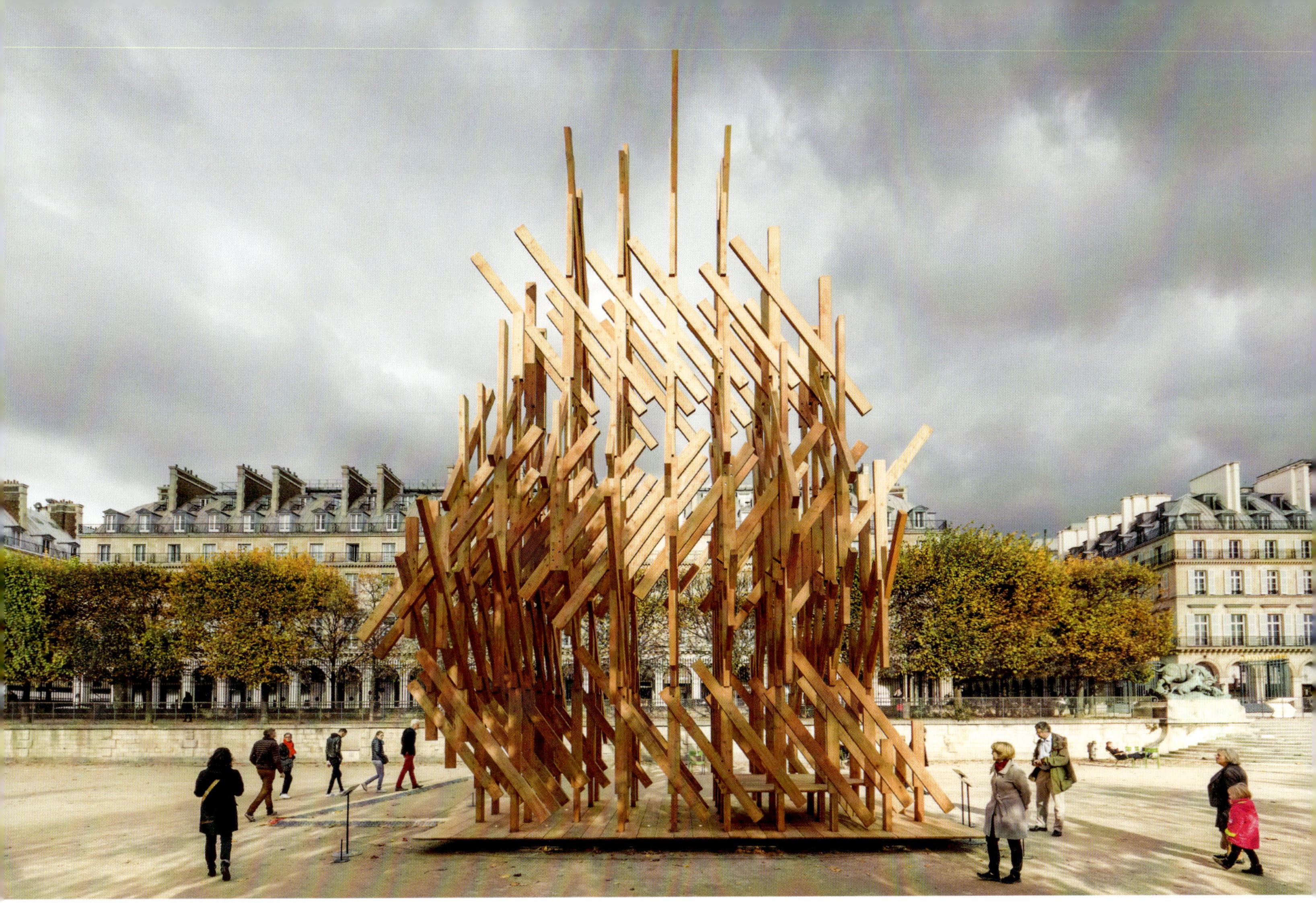

CIDORI

LOCATION Milan, Italy **COMPLETION** 2007
COLLABORATORS Kazuhiko Miyazawa
TYPOLOGY Cultural, Exhibition
PHOTOGRAPHY Kengo Kuma & Associates

LEGNO
DECODE ELEMENTS
Cidori
di/by KENGO KUMA
con/with Bals Tokyo e/and Motorola luce/light Targetti
INTERNI

Cidori, in Japanese, translates to 'a thousand birds' or 'plovers,' and it expresses and evokes the pattern and lightness of birds flying through the sky.

Cidori kōshi (or 'lattice') is a traditional technique used in the city of Hida Takayama to build wooden toys. Thin, rectangular pieces of wood are interlocked together with uniquely shaped notches in each piece. Each joint comprises three wood members, creating a strong structure without using any nails or adhesives, and that can be easy dismantled.

This joinery system became a source of inspiration and construction for our architectural conception for the Salone del Mobile 2007. We scaled up the method to fashion a voluminous three-dimensional space—an open and transparent pavilion that visitors can experience from inside and outside. The rigidity, intricacy, and infinite liberty of the lattice construction allowed for an eternally open pavilion that is as seemingly light as it is solid.

Cidori is an example of how we adapt ideas from experimental projects. A small toy became the inspiration for a pavilion in Milan, followed by the GC Prostho Museum Research Centre in Kasugai-shi, and a modular furniture system, using the same wooden components and unique joint.

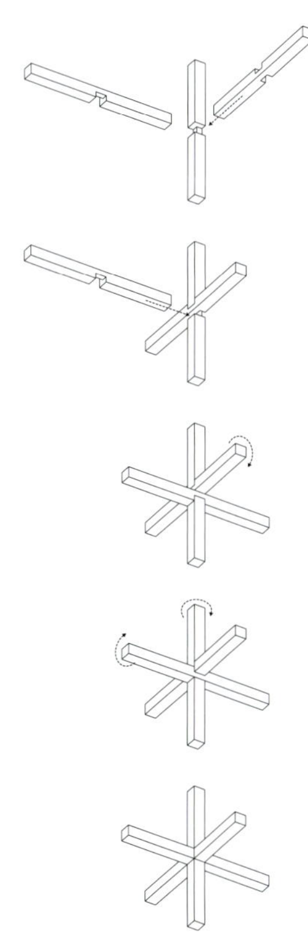

JOINT AXONOMETRIC

FRAME AXONOMETRIC

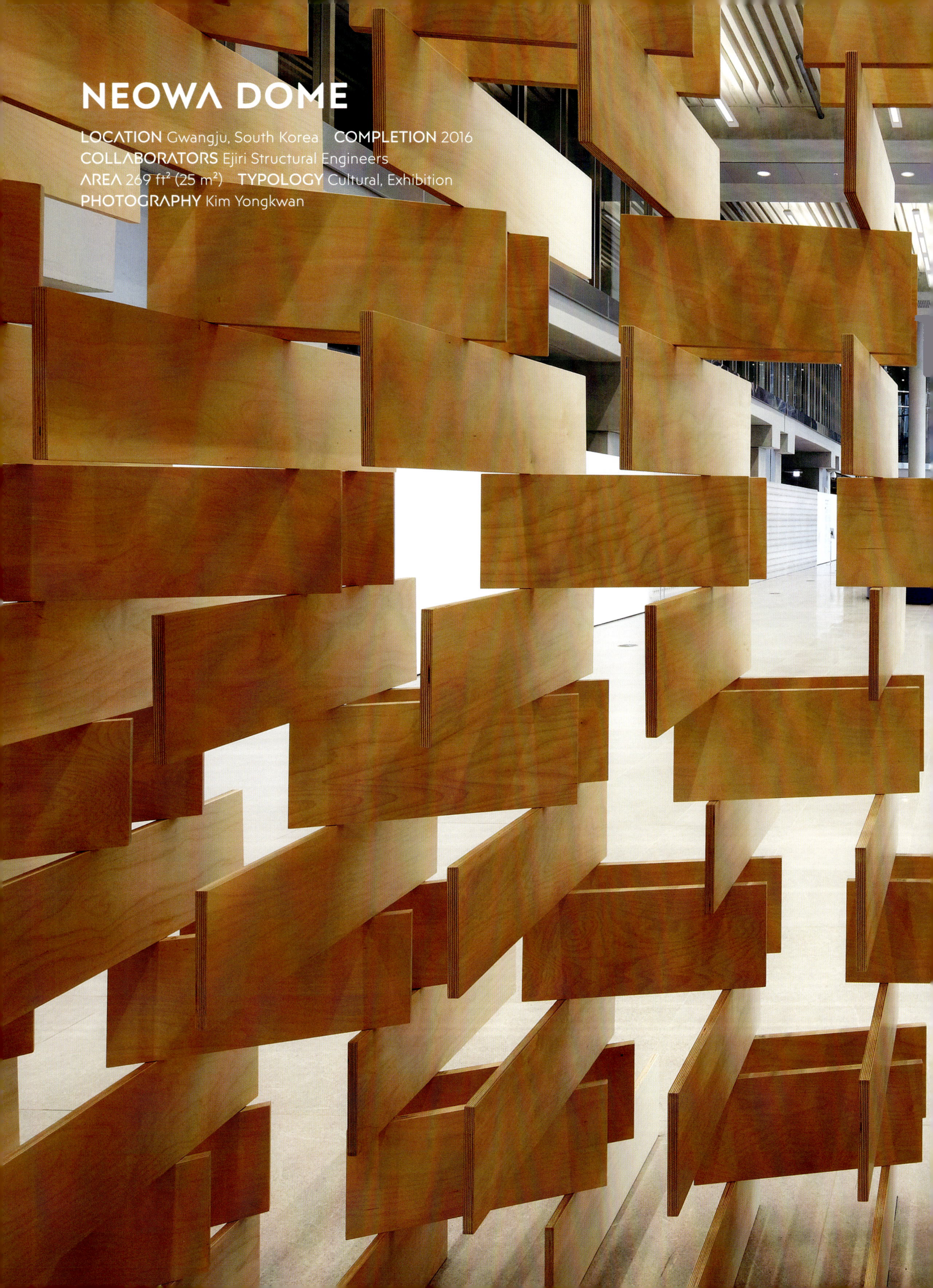

NEOWA DOME

LOCATION Gwangju, South Korea **COMPLETION** 2016
COLLABORATORS Ejiri Structural Engineers
AREA 269 ft² (25 m²) **TYPOLOGY** Cultural, Exhibition
PHOTOGRAPHY Kim Yongkwan

Neowa Dome is part of our exploration of democratic architecture, in which larger and larger structures can be crafted with the same small units, and it can be disassembled and remade into other structures and shapes.

Neowa is a shingle-style roof made with wooden slabs chopped with an axe, and has long been used for traditional Korean homes. For the National Asian Culture Center's permanent exhibition, we built Neowa Dome, a light and flexible pavilion constructed with the wooden slabs that have long formed a part of Korean housing.

The transparent dome, measuring 13.1 feet (4 meters) high and 19.7 feet (6 meters) in diameter, is made with perpendicular layers of birch plywood boards, becoming longer toward the top to create the dome. Stainless-steel dowel pins connect the boards, enabling the structure to be easily dismantled and transported. It can also be developed into other forms by changing the positions of the holes for connection.

KOMOREBI

LOCATION Saint Victoire, France **COMPLETION** 2017
COLLABORATORS Ejiri Structural Engineers
AREA 3,229 ft² (300 m²) **TYPOLOGY** Cultural, Exhibition
PHOTOGRAPHY Robin Oggiano; James Reeve

On the outskirts of Aix-en-Provence is Château La Coste, a wine estate and open-air museum with a view across the valley to Sainte-Victoire. This mountain was the subject of numerous artworks by Paul Cézanne, who painted it in watercolor and oil paint to capture the landscape with lightness and transparency. Transparency is key in creating a dialogue with nature.

For Château La Coste, we designed Komorebi, which translates to 'sunlight filtering through the foliage.' We sought to capture this poetically by creating a light, airy structure that coexists with nature. The organic shape evokes a tree, abstracted in the same way that Cézanne drew Sainte-Victoire.

We achieved a sense of lightness and transparency by gradually staggering boards of ipe, a dense South American wood. The 239 boards range from 4.9 feet (1.5 meters) long to 37.7 feet (11.5 meters) long. Stainless-steel plates placed between the timber planks support the cantilever and permeability of the structure. It appears to both emerge out of the earth and levitate above it, and sunlight filters between the timber boards.

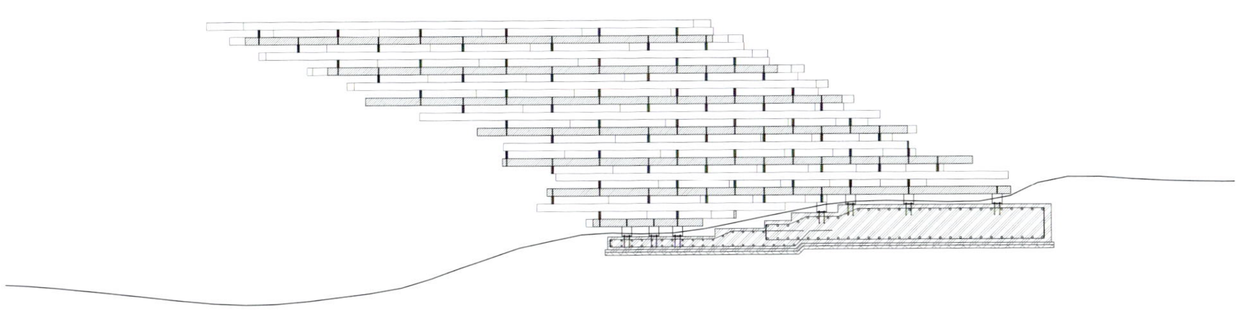

SECTION

BOTANICAL PAVILION

LOCATION Melbourne, Australia **COMPLETION** 2020
COLLABORATORS Ejiri Structural Engineers
CONSTRUCTION McCorkell Constructions Pty; Geoff Nees
AREA 678 ft² (63 m²) **TYPOLOGY** Cultural, Exhibition
PHOTOGRAPHY Earl Carter

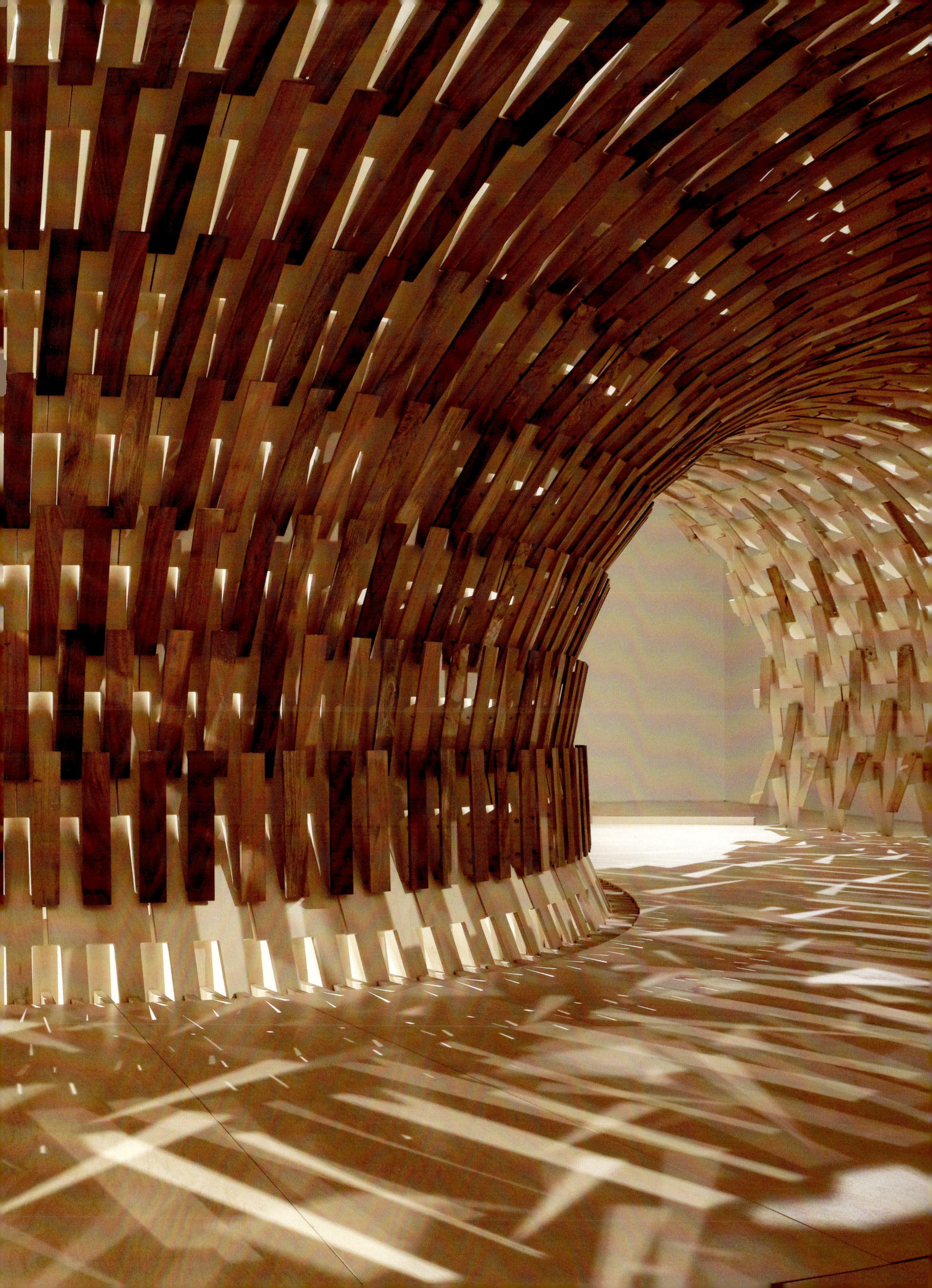

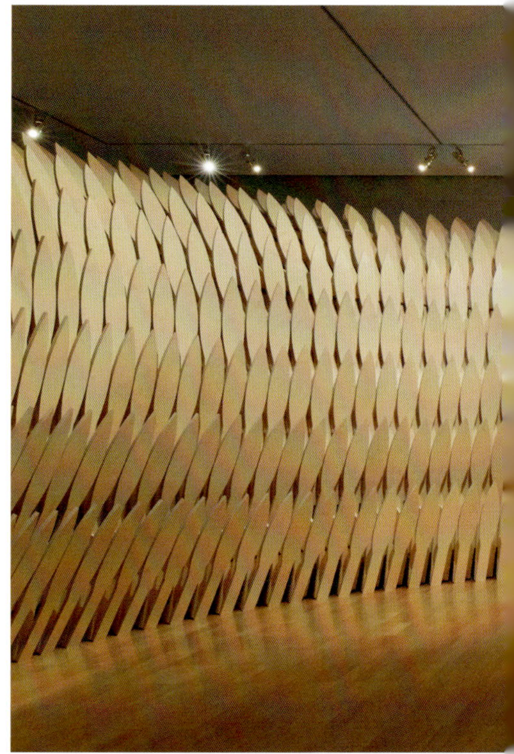

Botanical Pavilion was designed in collaboration with Australian artist Geoff Nees for the NGV Triennial 2020. The pavilion showcases timber collected from Melbourne's Royal Botanic Gardens, giving new life to the unused wood cut from felled or removed trees and displaying the beauty and qualities of different species.

The circular pavilion is made of wooden elements that interlock, like a puzzle, to form a structural arch. The tessellated, permeable form allows light and air to penetrate the porous wooden skin of the pavilion, creating a forest-like landscape.

The wooden elements in the pavilion are from different species of trees, which have their own unique properties, texture, and color. We catalogued the timber by color and produced a gradient in the pattern from darker to lighter to create a different perception of light and color throughout.

Visitors move through the circular pavilion experiencing the different types of wood and the light filtering through the structure. It is entirely recyclable and can be disassembled and reassembled in a different place.

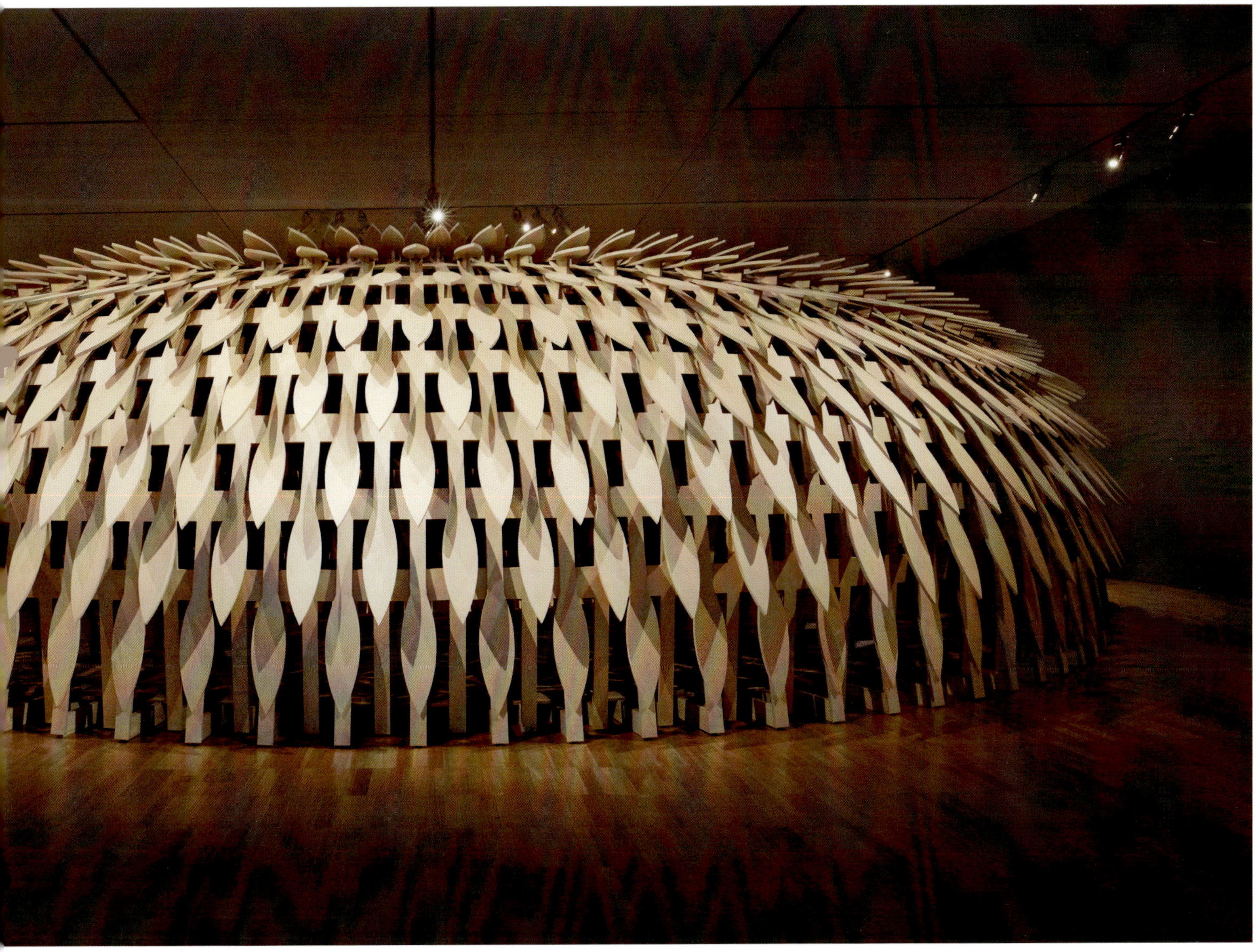

KODAMA

LOCATION Trento, Italy **COMPLETION** 2018
COLLABORATORS Jun Sato Structural Engineers
CONSTRUCTION D3 Wood **AREA** 269 ft^2 (25 m^2)
TYPOLOGY Cultural, Exhibition **PHOTOGRAPHY** Satoshi Asakawa

Respecting nature is an important aspect of many cultures and traditions, emphasizing a harmonious relationship with the natural environment. Arte Sella, the international contemporary art event staged in the beautiful forests of the Val di Sella in Trento, Italy, explores the relationship of people toward nature, and respect of nature inherently forms part of the artistic pieces.

For Arte Sella 2018, we created Kodama, which means 'echo,' with the intention of encouraging visitors' connection with nature and self-reflection. The 13-foot-high (4-meter-high) and nearly 20-foot-diameter (6-meter-diameter) spherical pavilion is made with an interlocking construction system using simple units of Japanese larch. The 335 jigsaw-like pieces each have three notches that interlock, enabling them to be assembled without using glue or metal fittings.

The message of Kodama is about circulation—what we believe to be the secret of nature. Using natural materials and creating forms that can be dismantled is part of the cycle of sustainable design.

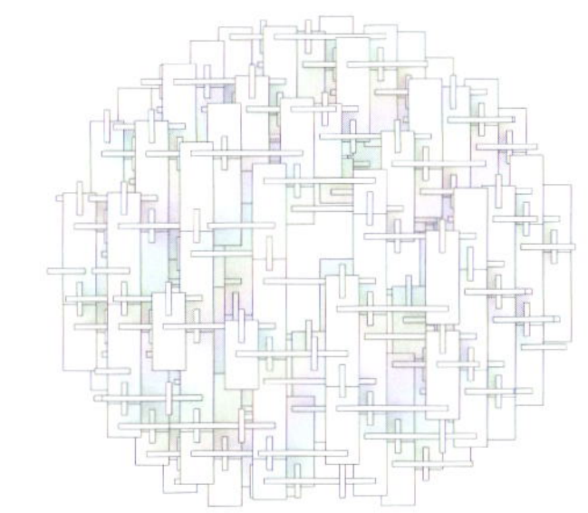

PLAN

ELEVATION FRONT

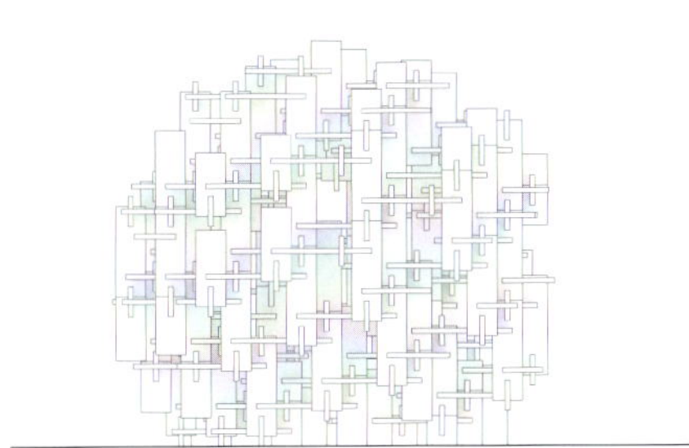

ELEVATION LEFT

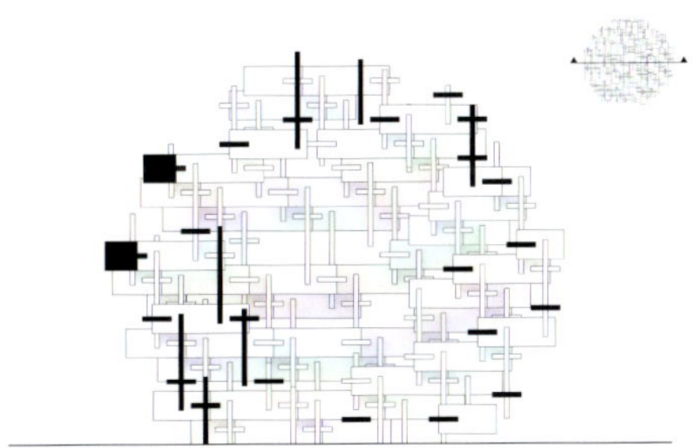

SECTION 1

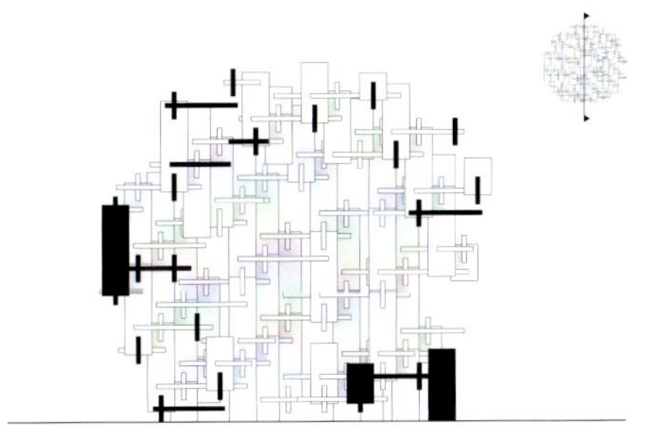

SECTION 2

CASA WABI COOP

LOCATION Oaxaca, Mexico **COMPLETION** 2018
TYPOLOGY Agricultural **PHOTOGRAPHY** Sergio Lopez

We conceived this chicken coop for the Casa Wabi Foundation in Puerto Escondido, Mexico, like we would a collective housing project: with private spaces for rest, communal spaces for gathering and eating, and outdoor spaces for all.

The gridded structure is built from 1.2-inch-thick (30-millimeter-thick) solid pine boards that have been charred following the traditional Japanese technique of *shou sugi ban*, providing a dark contrast to the white sand. It's constructed with a system of cross-lap jointed interlocking boards that creates lattice-like walls and roof that distribute the main structural loads across the building. For the horizontal loads, we inserted rigid elements within each of the lattice cells to avoid the typical structural bracing and maintain the gridded function and aesthetic.

The lattice walls and roof form a permeable structure that protects and ventilates the inhabitants. The individual cavities within the grid provide nooks for the chickens to rest, nest, and lay and incubate their eggs. In the center is a communal space for their general activities, such as gathering and eating.

The cavities in the gridded walls are covered with mesh or left open to allow a breeze and sunlight to pass through, while the wood slats provide shade. The permeable nature of this structure keeps the chickens cool and sheltered in the Mexican heat.

CLT PARK HARUMI

LOCATION Tokyo, Japan **COMPLETION** 2019
COLLABORATORS Ejiri Structural Engineers; Mitsubishi Estate Home; Mitsubishi Jisho Sekkei
OTHERS Denka; Device; Furukawa Company Group; Google; Iwai Corporation; Kazuhiro Kiriyama Architects; Makino Densetsu; Meiken Lamwood; Sentido; Stroog; TRA-K; Time & Style
TYPOLOGY Civic, Exhibition **PHOTOGRAPHY** Kawasumi Kobayashi Kenji Photograph Office

Information
消火栓

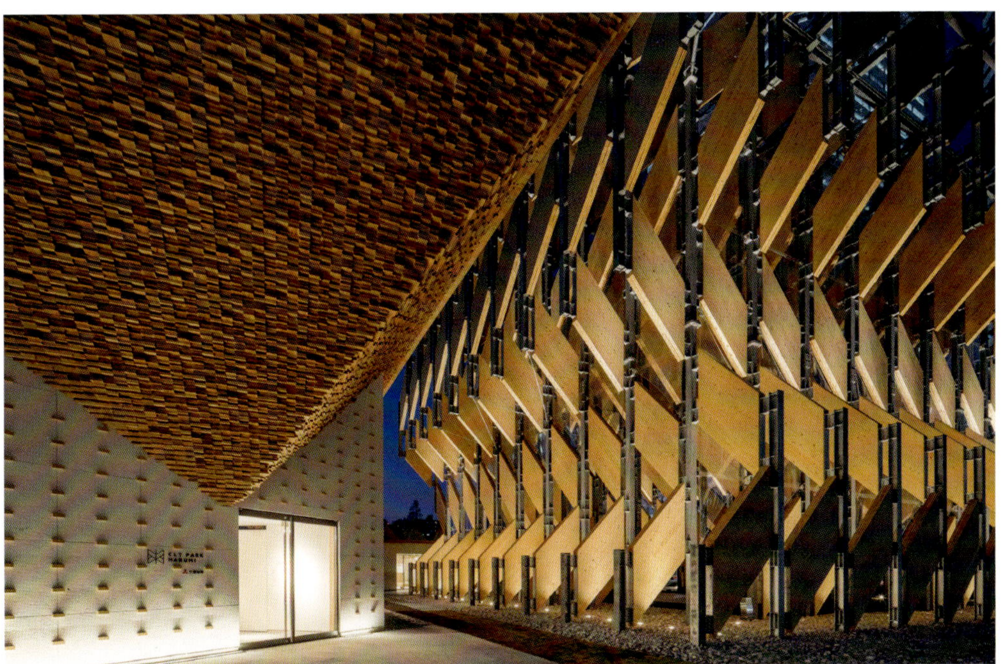

CLT Park Harumi was commissioned to display the versatility of Japanese cross-laminated timber (CLT), a strong and sustainable alternative to traditional construction. We designed the temporary pavilion in Harumi, Tokyo, to offer different opportunities for visitors to touch and interact with the material.

The building is made by weaving CLT leaves measuring 63 inches (160 centimeters) wide, 138 inches (350 centimeters) long, and 8.2 inches (21 centimeters) thick with a steel frame, creating a permeable structure that appears to spiral toward the sky. Transparent, kite-shaped pieces of TEFKA—a lightweight, pliable high-performance fluororesin film—seal the gaps between the CLT panels to protect the interior park and its visitors from rain and wind, while allowing light and ventilation to filter through the CLT leaves, like a tree canopy in a forest.

Two event spaces flank the pavilion. One features a staircase covered in a sweeping sculpture of stacked, perpendicular CLT planks.

The CLT panels are made with Japanese cypress from Maniwa city in Okayama Prefecture. Once the pavilion was dismantled, the panels were transported back to Maniwa and reassembled in Hiruzen Highland, where the wood was originally grown and harvested, serving as a model of the circular economy and connecting urban and rural areas.

EMACHU

WOODEN HAZE

LOCATION Singapore **COMPLETION** 2022
COLLABORATORS Alan Burden – Structured Environment
AREA 936 ft² (87 m²) **TYPOLOGY** Cultural, Exhibition
PHOTOGRAPHY Kengo Kuma & Associates; Potato Head; Studio Periphery

Wooden Haze is a structure that grows endlessly and eternally. We designed it for the *N*thing is Possible* exhibition at Singapore's National Design Centre, co-curated by OMA and Balinese hospitality brand Potato Head, our partner for waste material utilization projects in Bali. Presented as part of Singapore Design Week, the exhibition highlighted conscientious care for the environment in conjunction with design, celebrating the infinite possibilities of recycled materials.

The mission of *N*thing is Possible* was to demonstrate that zero waste and the experience of comfort and enjoyment are not mutually exclusive. Rather, waste can be reimagined into beautiful objects, functional furniture, and art.

To create Wooden Haze, we used waste wood that was processed into a cylindrical shape of different lengths: 19.4 inches (100 centimeters), 23.6 inches (60 centimeters), and 14.2 inches (36 centimeters). This formed three basic components that we combined in an endless, ever-growing wooden structure. Reminiscent of a molecular formula, it captures the boundless possibilities of recycled materials.

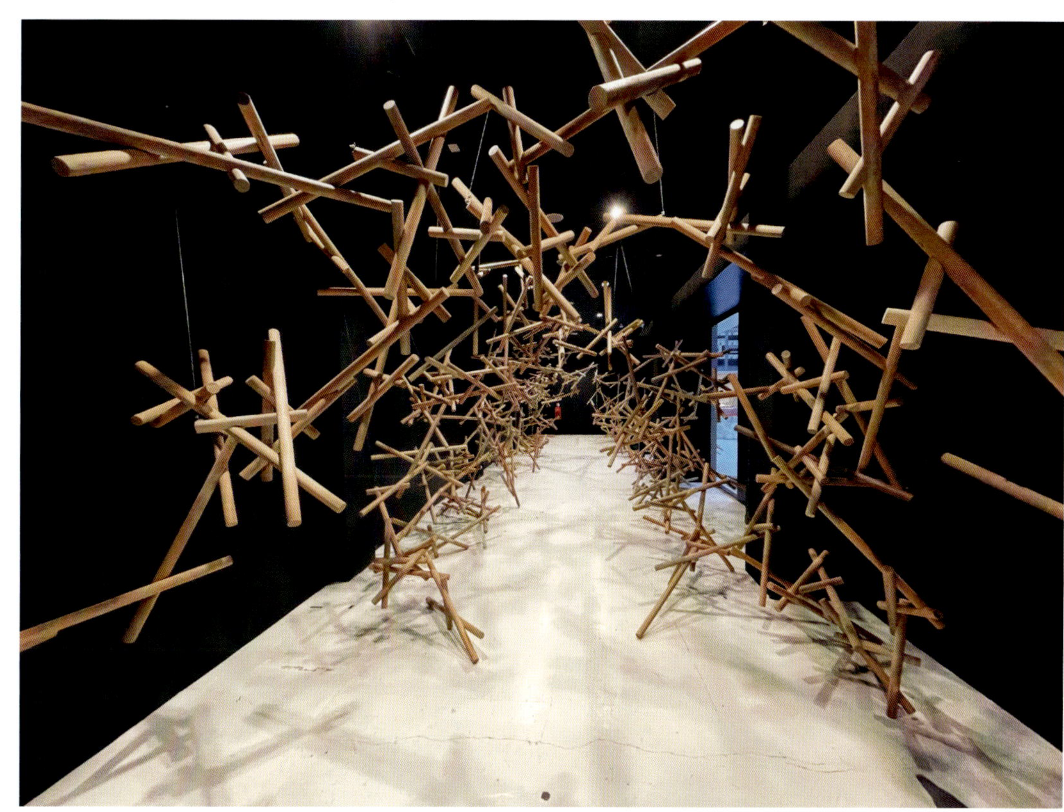

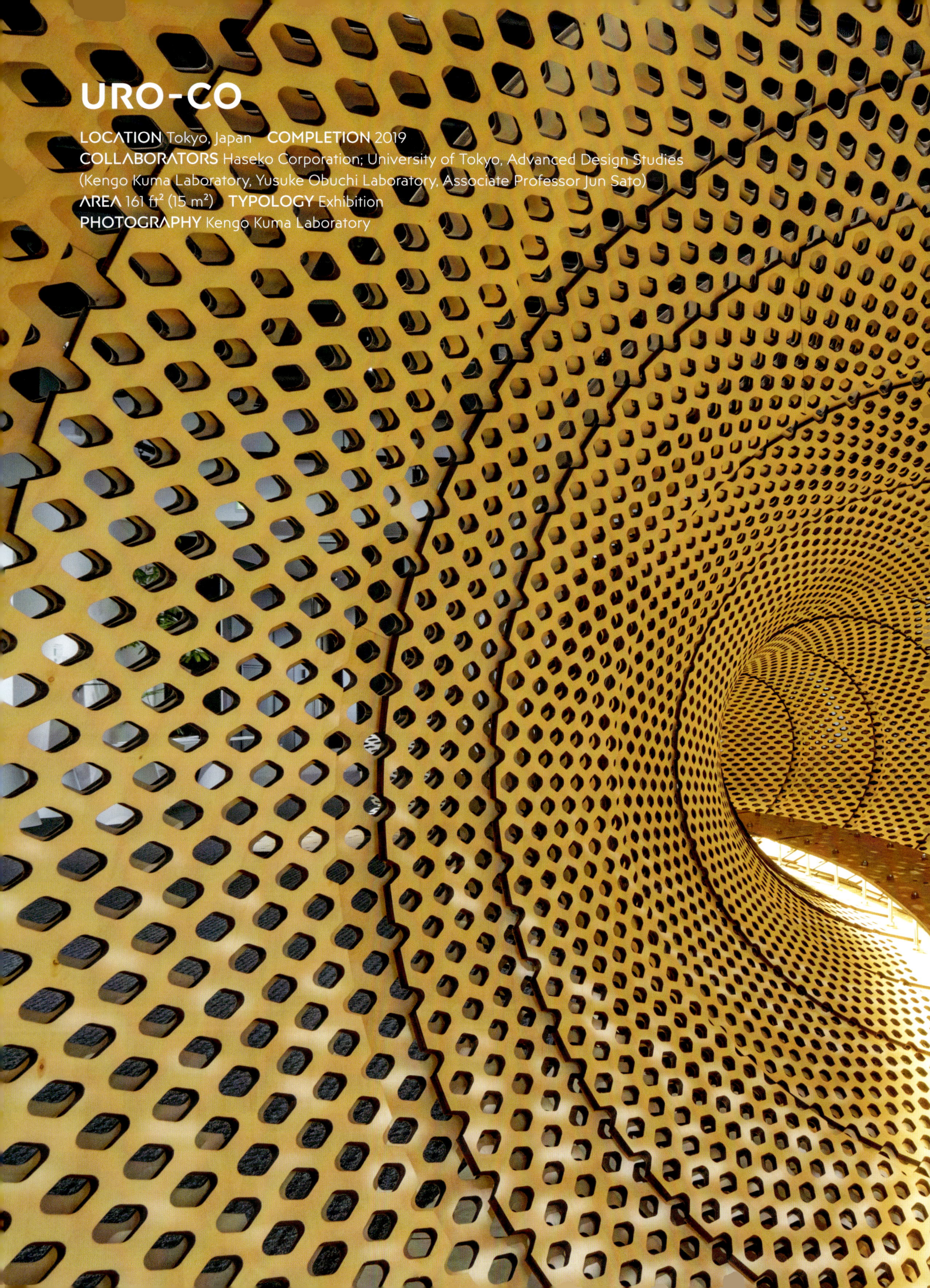

URO-CO

LOCATION Tokyo, Japan **COMPLETION** 2019
COLLABORATORS Haseko Corporation; University of Tokyo, Advanced Design Studies (Kengo Kuma Laboratory, Yusuke Obuchi Laboratory, Associate Professor Jun Sato)
AREA 161 ft^2 (15 m^2) **TYPOLOGY** Exhibition
PHOTOGRAPHY Kengo Kuma Laboratory

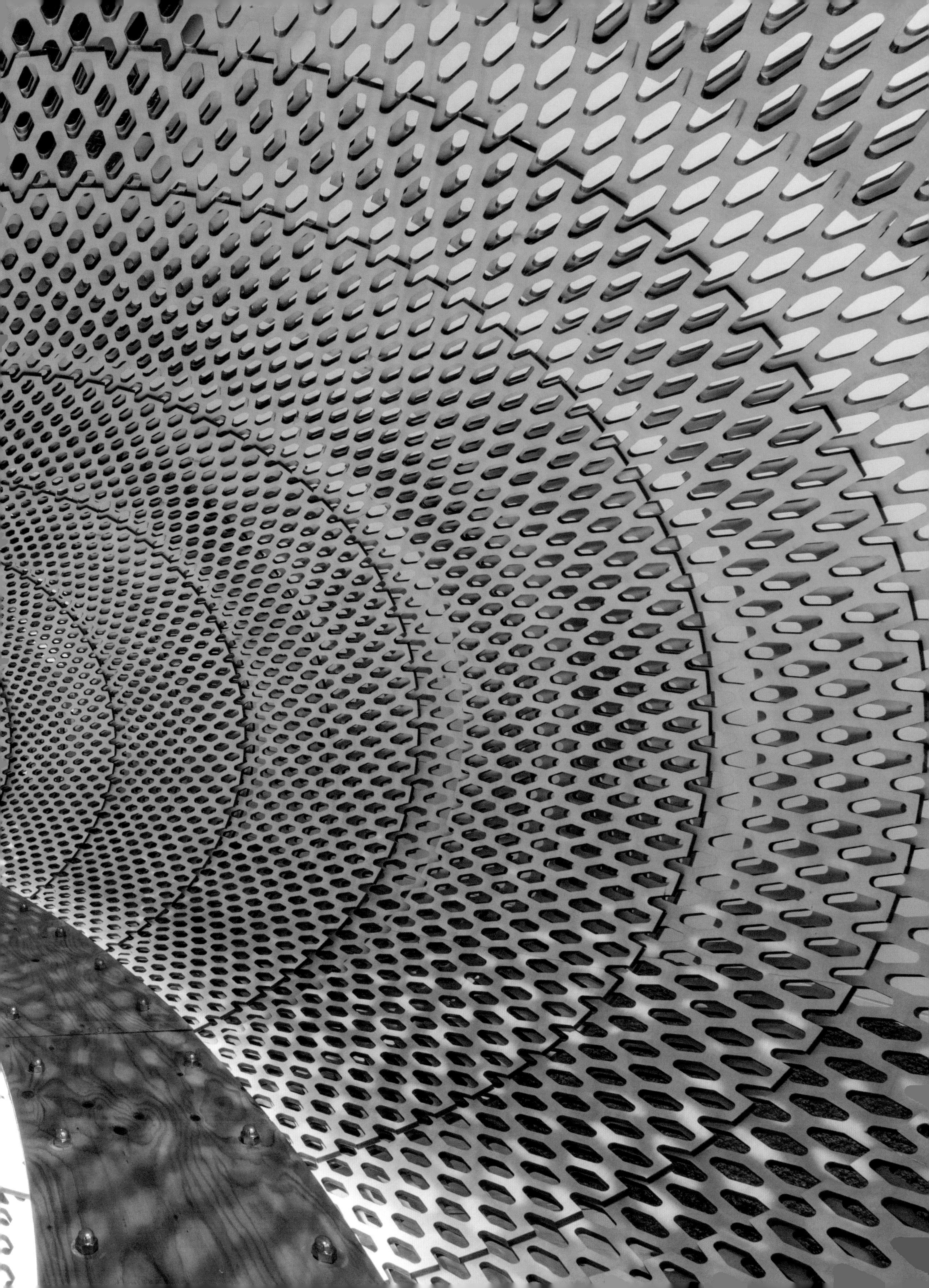

Uro-co experiments with the possibilities of plywood. Located inside LIPS (Living Image Presentation Space) at the office of the Japanese construction company Haseko Corporation, the pavilion explores the flexibility and rigidity of plywood and is both architecture and furniture.

The rounded form is achieved by laser cutting diamond-shaped perforations in the plywood, while still maintaining structural strength for it to serve as a seat. We calculated the ideal proportions and sizes of the perforations to achieve the flexibility and rigidity required.

The curving pavilion is made with a double layer of overlapping segmented pieces. Light filters in and out of the perforations, and an internal platform snakes through the middle, providing a crawl space.

We named the pavilion Uro-co, the Japanese word for 'fish scales,' for its diamond-shaped perforation patterns resembling scales and its overall fish-like shape.

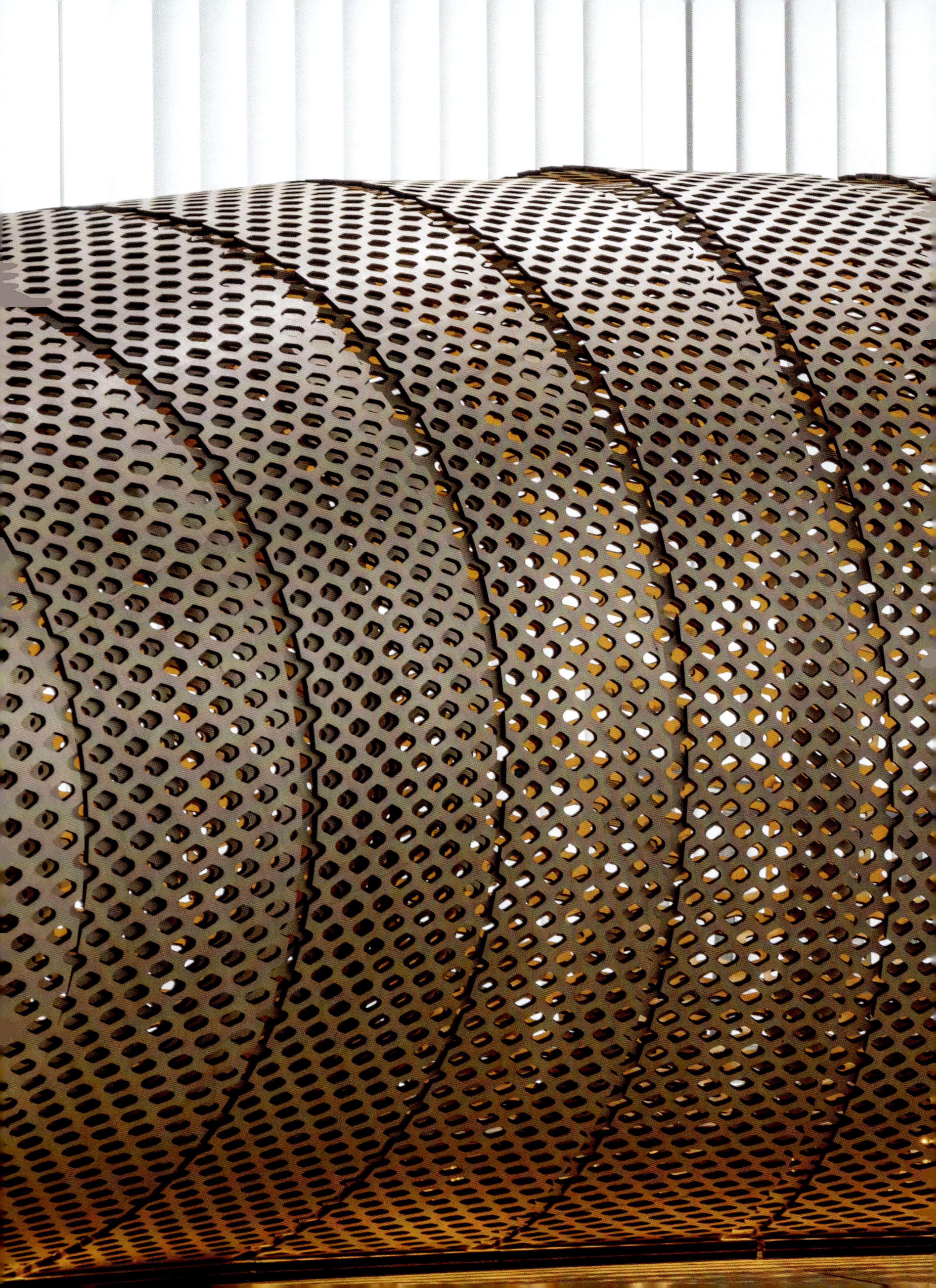

SANA MANE SAZAE SAUNA

LOCATION Kagawa, Japan **COMPLETION** 2022
COLLABORATORS ALG-Architectural Lighting Group; Ejiri Structural Engineers; Studio Nora **CONSTRUCTION** Sanyu Kenso **AREA** 86 ft² (8 m²)
TYPOLOGY Hospitality, Wellness **PHOTOGRAPHY** Keishin Horikoshi/SS

The island of Naoshima is known for its whimsical sculptures and installations, and buildings that translate architecture into large-scale immersive art. For the glamping resort of Sana Mane, we designed the sauna as a mollusk-like organic structure, giving it a sculptural presence, befitting of the rich artistic and architectural character of the island.

Sazae Sauna—*sazae* being the Japanese name for the mollusk *Turbo cornutus*—sits amid geodesic cottages. Drawing inspiration from its coastal context, the organic structure bulges at the bottom, spiraling upward to appear like an enlarged shell, sitting upright on the shore.

The sauna is formed with 150 layers of 1.1-inch-thick (28-millimeter-thick) plywood. We used a CNC machine to cut 1,500 plywood sheets into 5,000 pieces. These were assembled on-site like a puzzle, resulting in the intricately pleated and textured volume that shape-shifts from different vantage points. Inside and outside, there is a play of light and shadow across the intricate folds and undulations.

Natural light filters through an oculus in a dramatic yet meditative manner, lending a sacred character to the sauna. The surfaces of the wooden layers expand into the cave-like interior to become circulation spaces and curvaceous seating.

Normally, a space with such a high ceiling would not be suitable for a sauna. Sazae Sauna has forced ventilation with intake from the top and exhaust from the bottom. The average wall thickness of 17.7 inches (45 centimeters) ensures heat insulation and retention.

ELEVATION

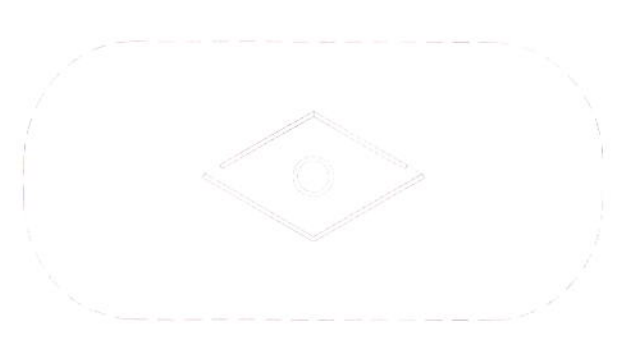

DETAIL

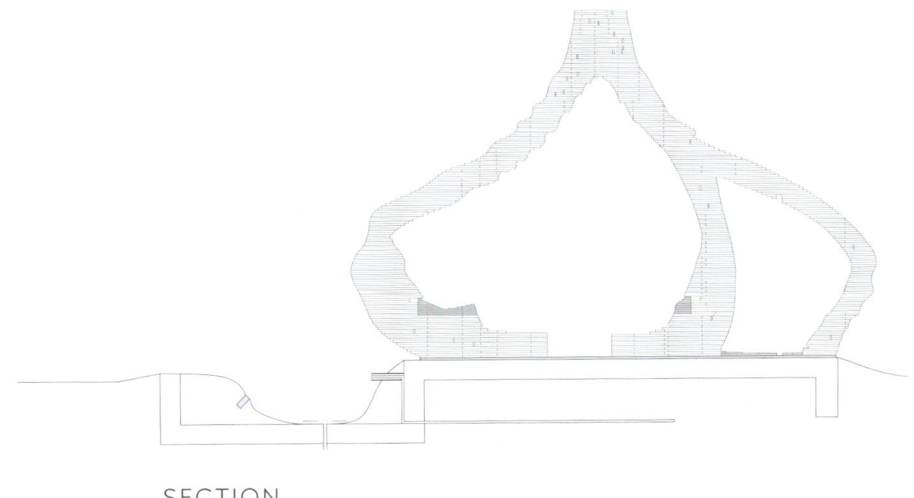

SECTION

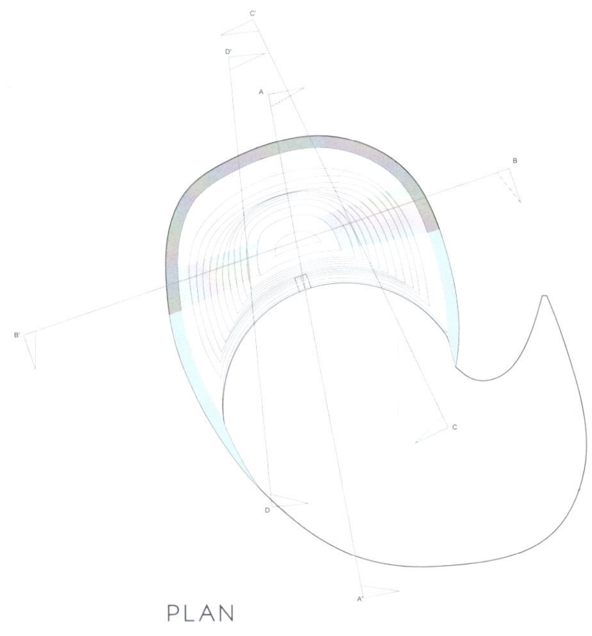

PLAN

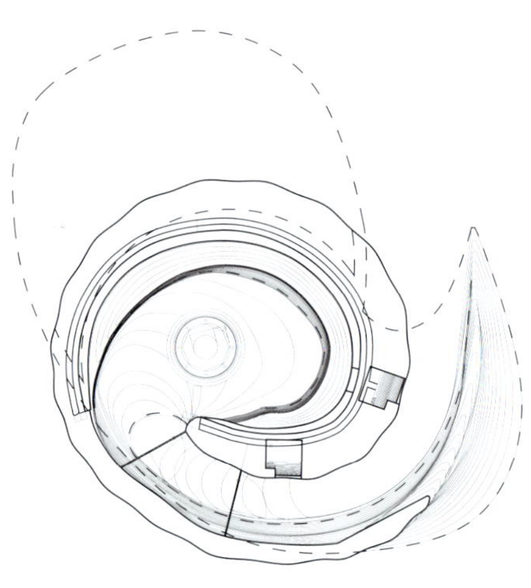

PLAN SECTION

NAKAHASHI

LOCATION Miyagi, Japan **COMPLETION** 2019
COLLABORATORS Oak Structural Design; Pacific Consultants
TYPOLOGY Infrastructure
PHOTOGRAPHY Keishin Horikoshi · Kosuke Nakao / SS Tokyo

Nakahashi is a footbridge commemorating the restoration efforts of Minamisanriku, a small coastal town that was heavily impacted by the Tōhoku earthquake and tsunami that devastated northeastern Japan in March 2011.

We designed the 262-foot-long (80-meter-long) pedestrian bridge as a place of prayer. Traversing the Hachiman River, it connects Minamisanriku Earthquake Disaster Memorial Park to the bustling Minamisanriku Sun Sun Shopping Village and leads to Kaminoyama Hachiman shrine. In Japan, bridges along the path to the shrine serve to divide and connect the ordinary world to the divine realm.

The bridge has a gentle arch, like a typical *taikobashi*—an arched pedestrian bridge leading to a shrine. The arch of Nakahashi is mirrored, creating a lenticular truss structure spanning the length of the bridge. While the upper chord arches up and creates a footpath with a view toward the ocean, the lower chord dips toward the surface of the river. The intricately connected arches offer two different views and experiences of the bridge.

The steel structure has wooden decking made with cedar from the former Shizugawa Station in Minamisanriku. This combination of materials prevents structural deformation and brings a warm, natural aesthetic to the coastal town. Tall wooden columns along the approach to the lower footbridge connect the gap between the mirrored arches. Locals have come to view this column arcade like Senbon Torii—*torii* being the traditional gateway at the entrance of Shintō shrines.

中橋
なかはし

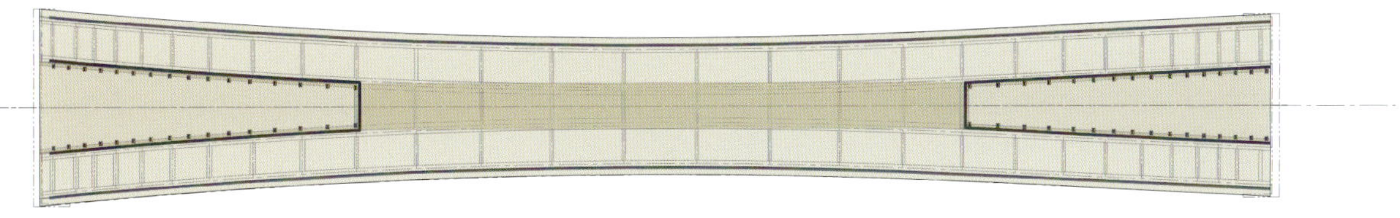

PLAN

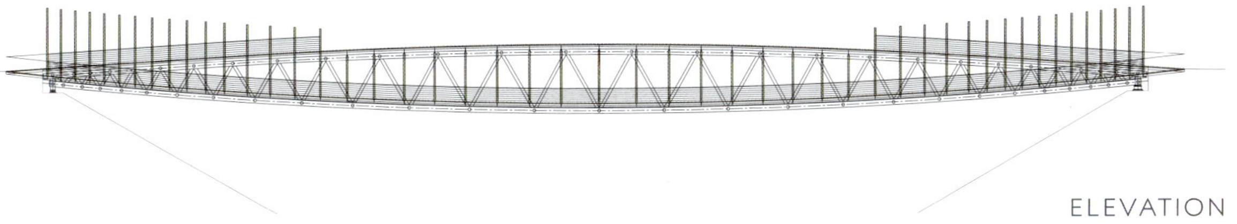

ELEVATION

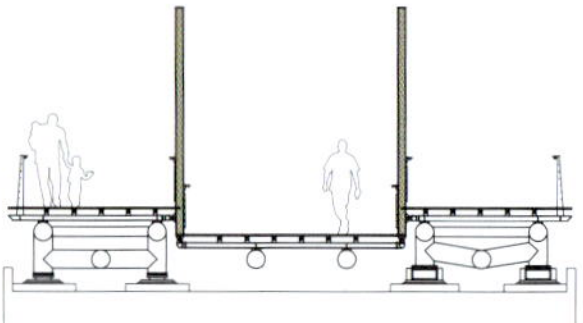

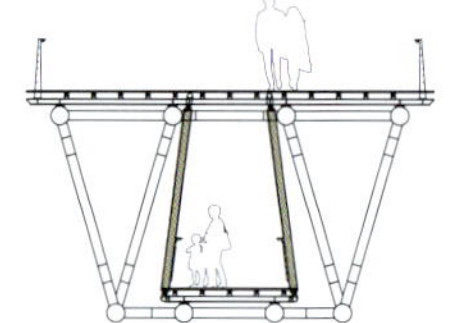

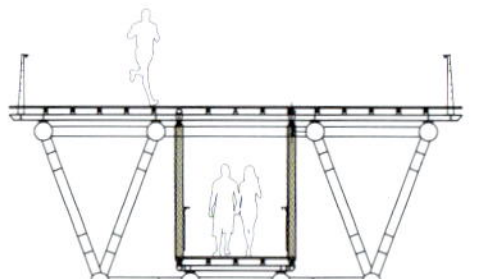

SECTION

KUSUGIBASHI

LOCATION Iwakuni City, Japan **COMPLETION** 2022
COLLABORATORS Nichiei Kogyo; Yuri Kensetsu Kogyo; OAKplus
AREA 5,686 ft^2 (528 m^2) **TYPOLOGY** Infrastructure
PHOTOGRAPHY Katsumasa Tanaka

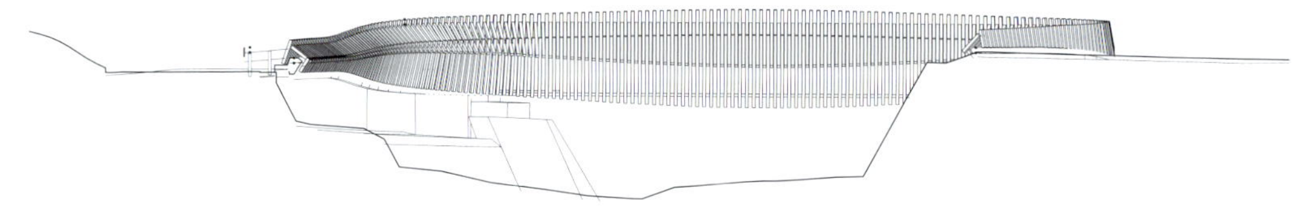

ELEVATION

After the original bridge in Osogoe, Shuto Town, Iwakuni City, was destroyed by the floods in 2018, we designed a wooden bridge that would become a new symbol for the community. By combining Japan's carpentry skills with the modern technology of computational design, we achieved a soft and human expression in civil infrastructure.

Considering the risk of recurring disasters, a reinforced concrete frame was combined with square cypress balustrades. The balustrades are arranged in a gentle curve that echoes the contour of the surrounding mountain range and embraces the sides of the road. We used 4.2-inch (105-millimeter) square components—the most common size in Japanese wooden construction—to create a bridge that felt familiar and nostalgic and had a human scale.

The elaborate structure showcases the subtlety and elegance of timber and serves as a symbol of renewal for the local community. To each side of the bridge are the Dassai store and brewery that sells a Japanese sake created by Asahi-Shuzo brewery, which donated the wood for the bridge's construction.

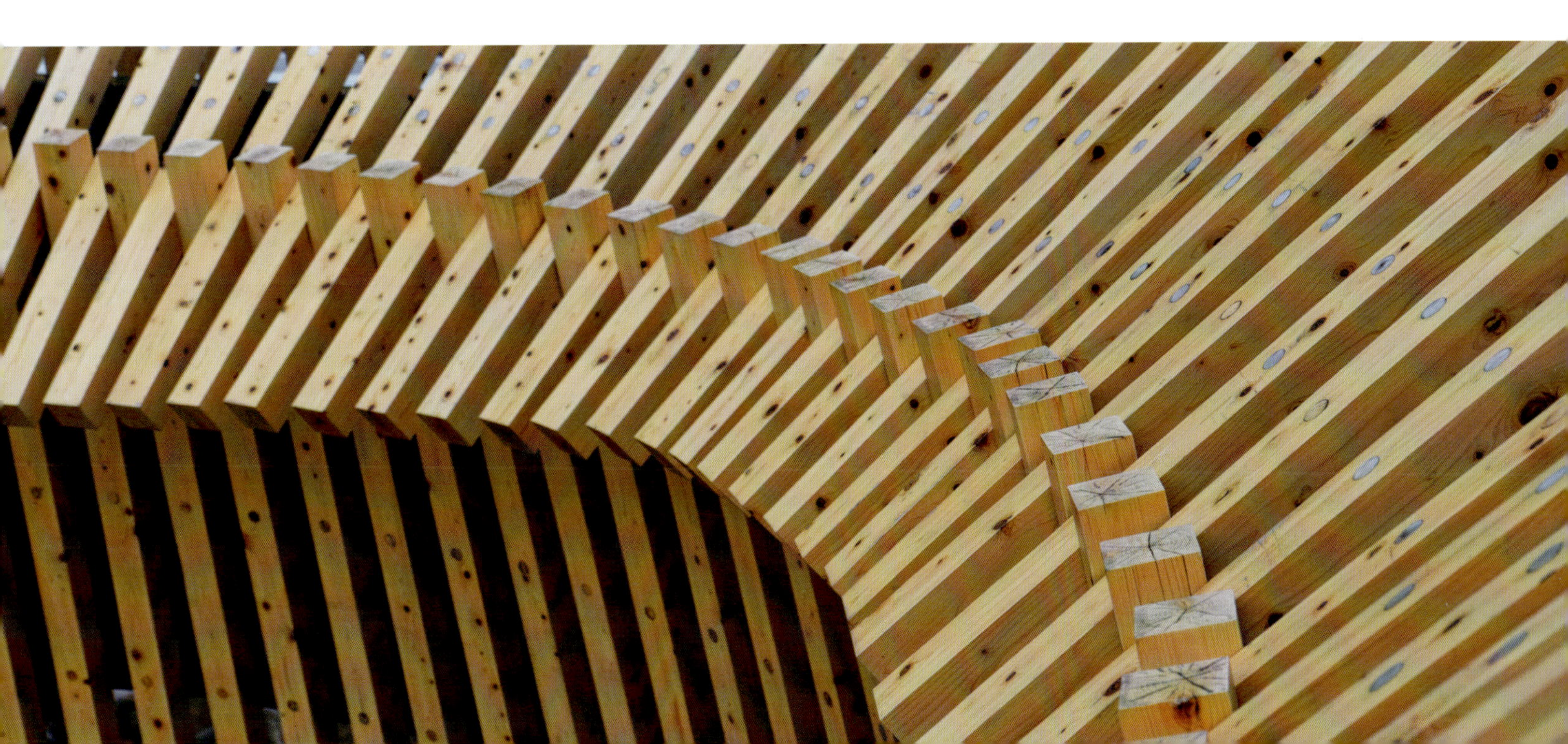

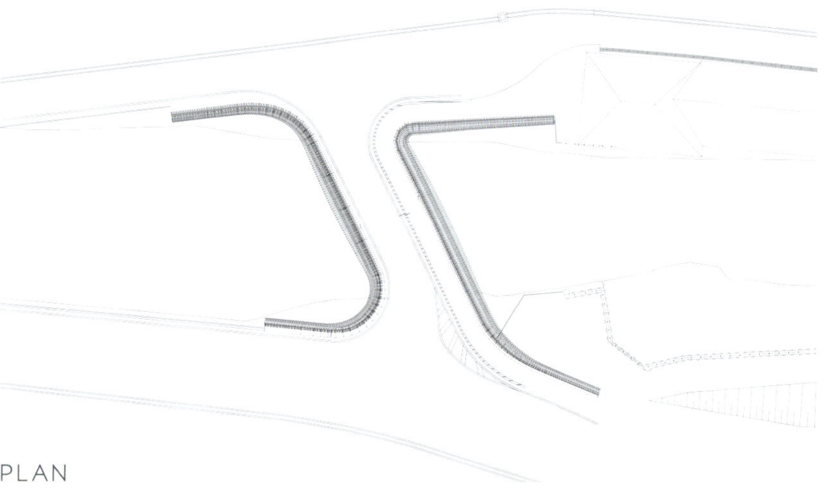

PLAN

BAMBOO

NANGCHANG-NANGCHANG

LOCATION Guangju, South Korea **COMPLETION** 2013
CONSTRUCTION Mr. Hwang In-jin **ILLUMINATION** Bitzro
AREA 775 ft² (72 m²) **TYPOLOGY** Cultural, Exhibition
PHOTOGRAPHY Kengo Kuma & Associates

In my architecture, I am always attempting to connect people with the buildings they spend time in. For the 2013 Gwangju Design Biennale, we used the warmth, tactility, and flexibility of bamboo to foster this closer relationship between humans and architecture. The Nangchang-Nangchang pavilion's wave-like form invites visitors to recline and embraces people as they walk over or its springy surfaces, producing a subtle vibration as they do.

We split the bamboo into 1.18-inch-wide (3-millimeter-wide) strips to make it easy to bow and bend into walkways and seating areas. The bamboo strips are attached along two edges of a fixed base, and the reeds push against each other where they meet in the middle, causing one side to curl back on itself and the other to flow over the top. The curves create seating areas that visitors can recline against, while the upper strands gently fold and splay over the base to form a covered, tunnel-like walkway.

A series of alternating sections provided a 65.5-foot-long (20-meter-long) passage between two exhibition halls at the Biennale. Inside one of the galleries, staggered sections provided small pockets of seating space, and lighting from below illuminated the splaying strands.

SENSING SPACES

LOCATION London, United Kingdom **COMPLETION** 2014
COLLABORATORS Ejiri Structural Engineers
TYPOLOGY Cultural, Exhibition **PHOTOGRAPHY** Manhole

Continuing to reinforce this connection between people and buildings, I see architecture as a full body and sensory experience. For the *Sensing Spaces: Architecture Reimagined* exhibition at London's Royal Academy of Arts, we designed a pavilion that would induce maximum effect on a body through the minimum amount of material: the less material, the larger the void, the more sensitive we become to it. The Japanese tea house embodies this principle of minimizing materials and maximizing sensory qualities.

We created an intricate, transparent tea house infused with scent. The 16.4-foot-high (5-meter-high) structure is made with bamboo whittled to 0.16-inch (4-millimeter) diameter, realized with modern technology. The delicate material is imbued with the aroma of tatami mats—a reminder of our childhood homes in Japan.

The bamboo was specially imported from Kyoto and had matured for four years, making it more supple to bend, and able to absorb and slowly release fragrances. The strands were gently illuminated with LED lights at their base, creating an ethereal quality.

In traditional Japanese architecture, the void—or *ma*—is the most important space. More than simply empty space, the void holds potential and significance and is central to the Japanese concept of appreciating the spaces between things. The void is also a sensor; it's the space between, where you can feel the change of light, time, smell, and temperature.

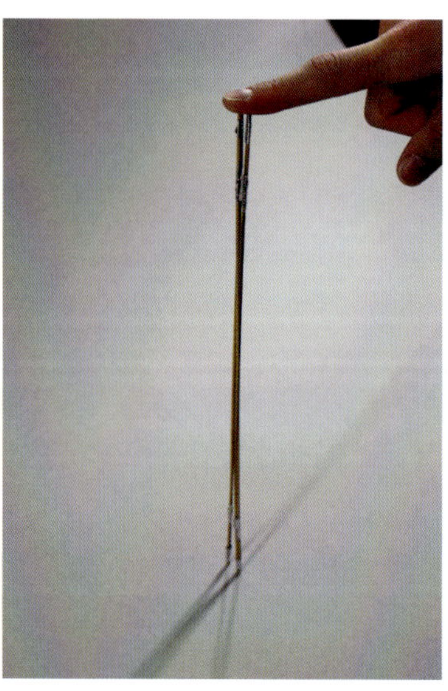

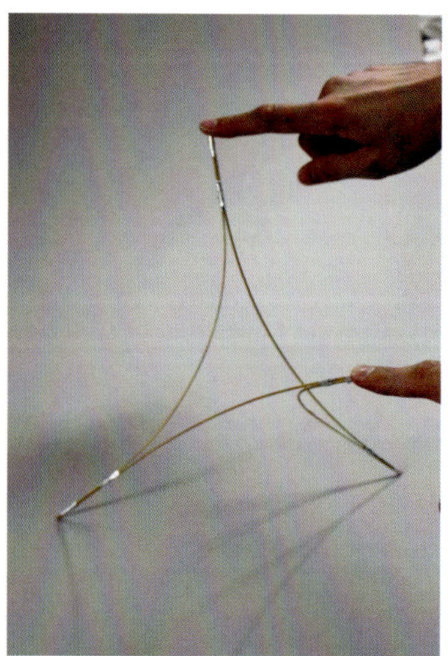

BAMBOO PASSAGE

LOCATION Beijing, China **COMPLETION** 2022
TYPOLOGY Cultural, Exhibition
PHOTOGRAPHY CreatAR; Kengo Kuma & Associates; Zhu Yumeng

Bamboo Passage is an immersive path that connects the ordinary and the extraordinary, welcoming visitors to our touring exhibition in China and heightening their anticipation for the sensory experience ahead.

Architecture for the Five Senses showcased our post-pandemic proposal of experiencing and interacting with architecture through the lens of the five human senses: sight, hearing, smell, taste, and touch.

Visitors enter the gallery through Bamboo Passage that evoked the sense of a tunnel piercing through a bamboo grove. The intricate installation is made with 10,000 flat bamboo pieces, each 0.6 inches (15 millimeters) wide and 0.1 inches (3 millimeters) thick, connected with renewable, readjustable joints.

The softness and weight of the bamboo form a subtle tension, as the reaction force and load gently curve the bamboo pieces. The organic space frame created ensures the stability of the structure and invites visitors to walk through the passage and touch the frame.

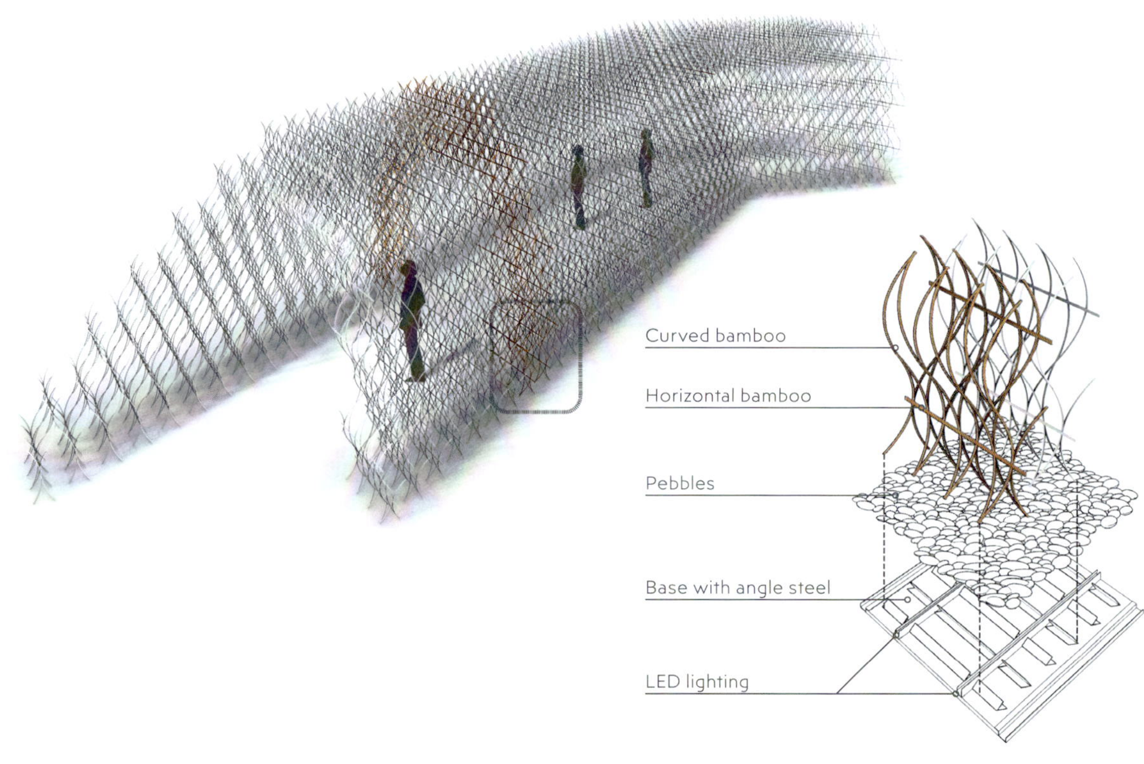

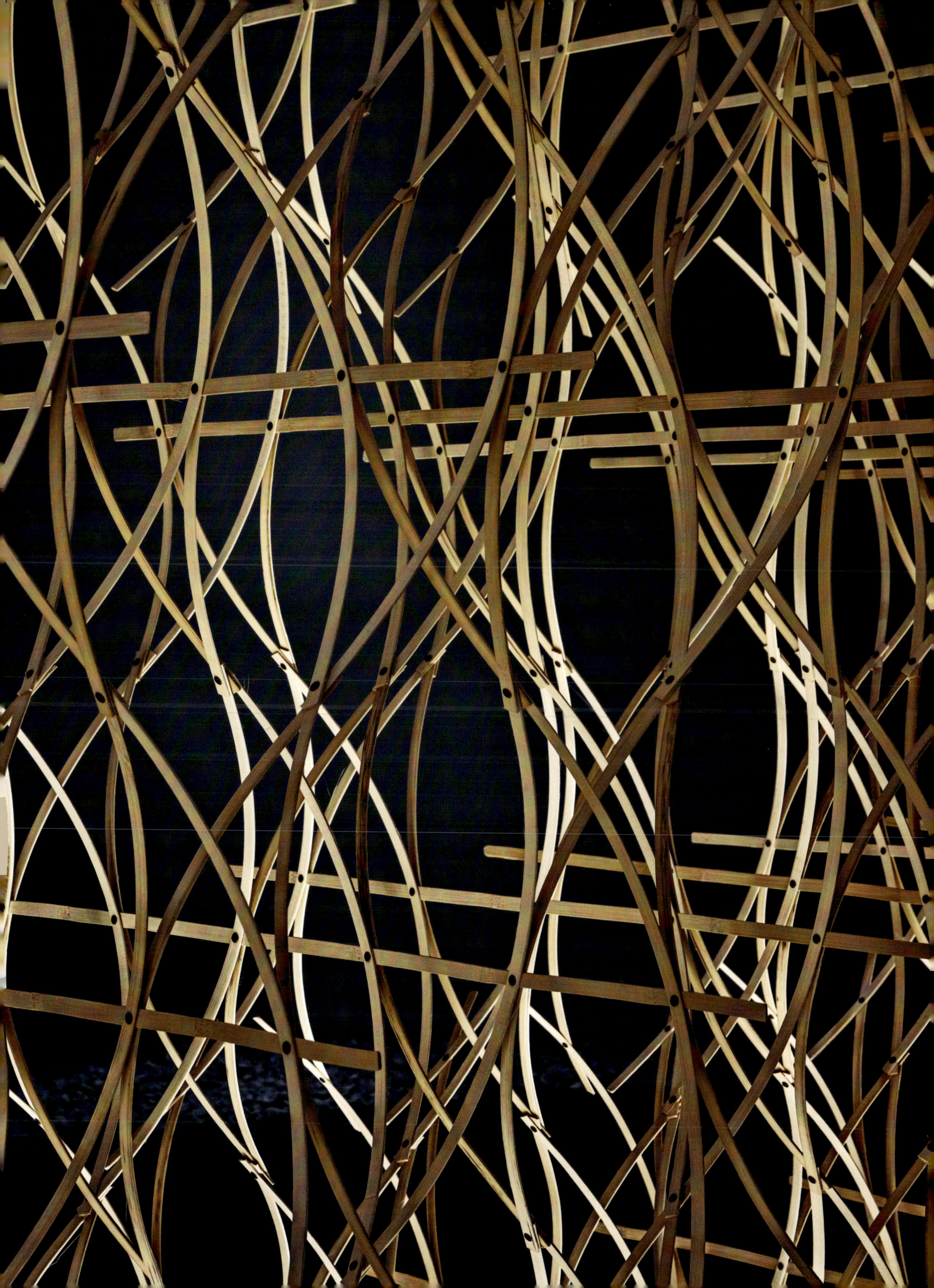

BAMBOO FLOW

LOCATION Beijing, China **COMPLETION** 2022
TYPOLOGY Cultural, Exhibition, Tea House
PHOTOGRAPHY CreatAR; Zhu Yumeng

Inside the exhibition hall of *Architecture for the Five Senses*, we constructed Bamboo Flow as a tea house amid a tranquil bamboo grove. We wanted to generate a quieter, garden-like space in dynamic contrast to the main circulation.

The tea house is a spiraling form of three-dimensional screens made with curving bamboo strips measuring 2 inches (5 centimeters) wide and 0.8 inches (2 centimeters) wide. The bamboo pieces are fixed to small wooden components that are attached to the end of fork-shaped steel plates consisting of arms with different lengths. With all the different bamboo curvatures, the tea house has an organic randomness and a whirlpool-like effect.

Bamboo Flow embodies the beauty of the 'noise' in Asian art, such as the 'faint' and 'blur' of calligraphy and the sounds of musical instruments, which cannot be achieved with industrialized methods and materials.

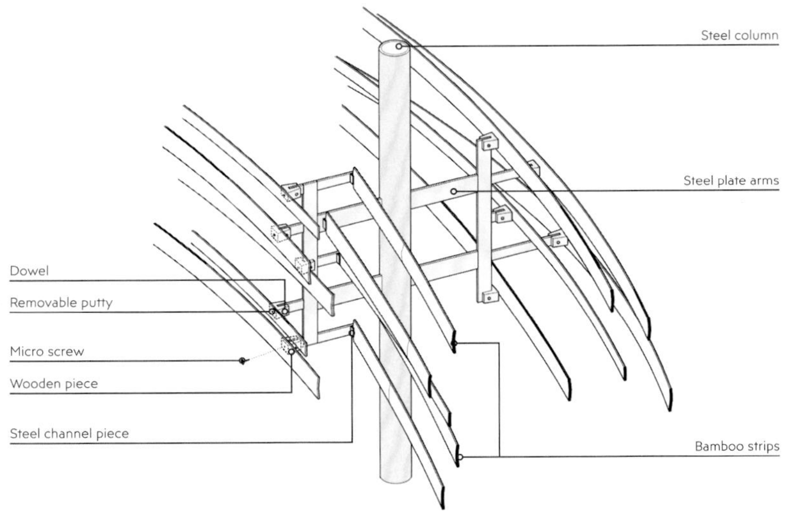

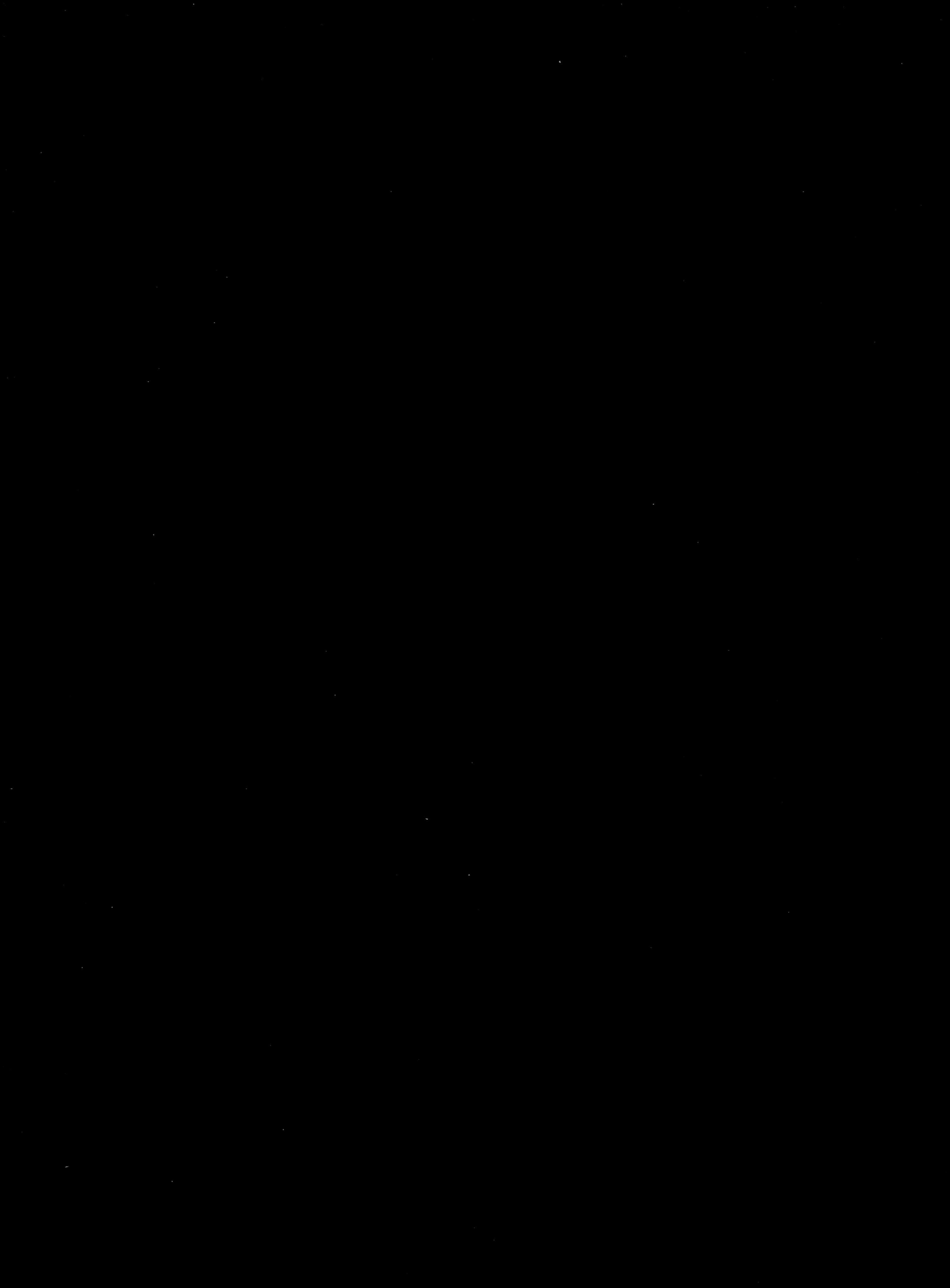

METAL

ONE HEALTH CARBON GATE

LOCATION Fukuoka, Japan **COMPLETION** 2022
COLLABORATORS Architainment Inc.; Azusa Sekkei; Ejiri Structural Engineers; Oh-Yabu Construction **TYPOLOGY** Civic, Cultural
PHOTOGRAPHY Kawasumi Kobayashi Kenji Photograph Office

Located alongside Yabe River, Chikugo Regional Park in Fukuoka Prefecture embraces its rich, natural environment and has been designed based on the principles of nature, culture, lifestyle, health, and interaction.

For the main entrance of the park, we designed a soaring, spiral-shaped monument that arches from one side of the road and back again. We aimed to realize the World Health Organization's concept of One Health, which recognizes that the health of humans is closely connected to the health of animals and our shared environment.

The distinctive shape is made using braided 0.6-inch-diameter (15-millimeter-diameter) eco-friendly carbon fiber tubes that have been formed into a double helix and wrapped into a torus. By lifting two sides of the torus, it becomes a double arch, like a Möbius loop. Steel rods, measuring one third of a circle's circumference, connect the spiraling form at twenty-nine different optimized angles, helping reduce the cost and the construction period.

Instead of a monumental gate, the light, soft, spiraling structure rests gently on the land. It harmonizes with the river, parkland, and sky, and allows a breeze to flow through.

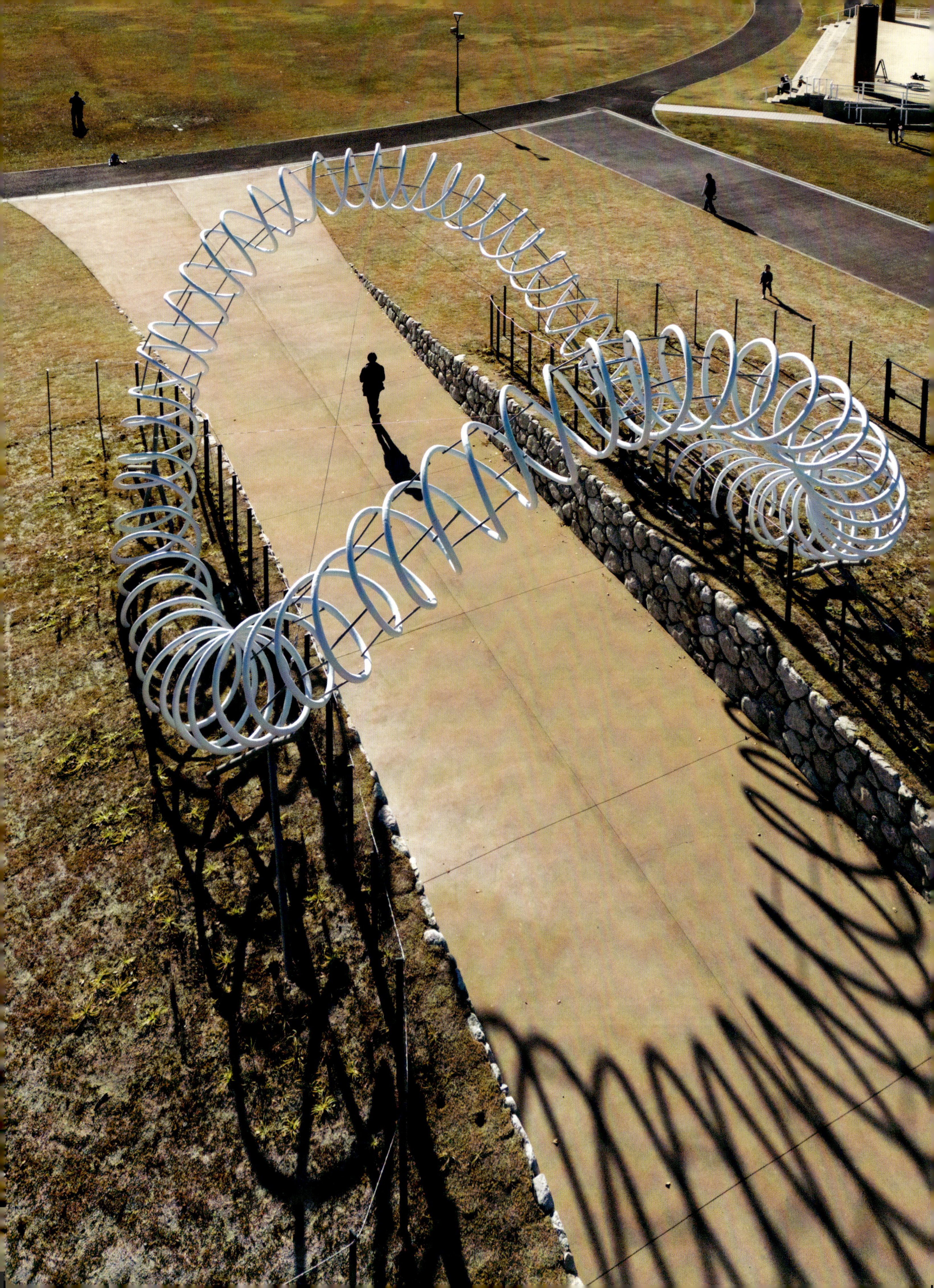

OWAN

LOCATION Basel, Switzerland **COMPLETION** 2016
TYPOLOGY Cultural, Exhibition **PHOTOGRAPHY** Kengo Kuma & Associates

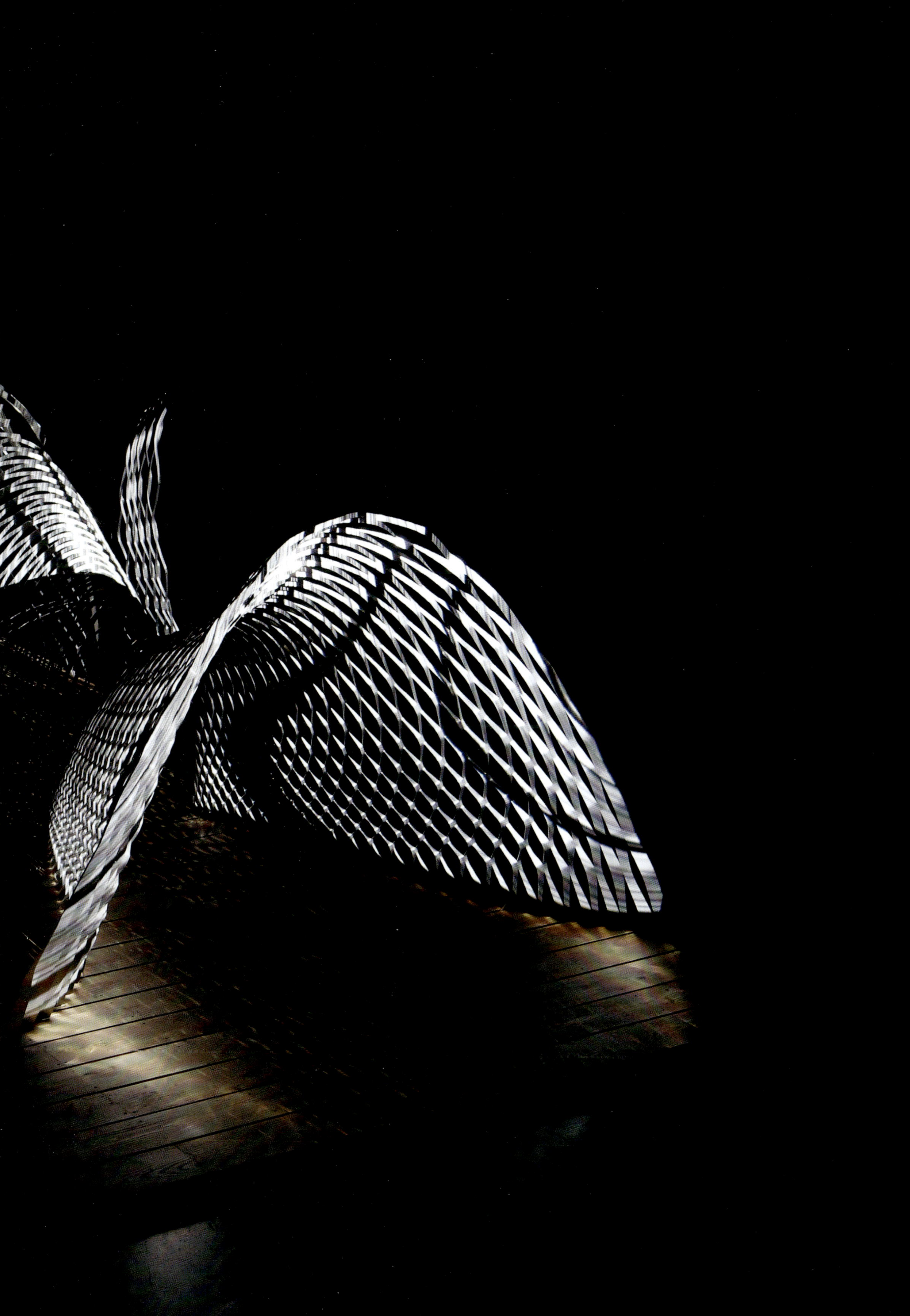

We designed Owan for Galerie Philippe Gravier's ongoing *Small Nomad House* series, this time for Design Basel/ Miami 2016. Seeking to create a harmonious relationship between architecture and landscape, the curving, zigzag-shaped dwelling merges interior and exterior space and introduces a variety of spatial experiences for those within it.

Drawing from the aesthetic of fish scales and traditional Japanese tea bowls, the metal shell has an unclear, undulating, and adjustable edge that allows it to seamlessly blend with its environment and makes it light enough to gently move in the wind.

The structurally malleable framework is made with a 0.08-inch-thick (2-millimeter-thick) shape-memory alloy that allows the form to warp and bend to a desired, manipulated position upon application of heat. Though appearing porous, *Owan* is lined with a thin, waterproof membrane that can move with the lightweight structure.

Owan is easily transportable and can transform from a two-dimensional form into a three-dimensional universe.

CASA BATLLÓ STAIRS

LOCATION Barcelona, Spain **COMPLETION** 2021
COLLABORATORS Viabizzuno
AREA 2,799 ft² (260 m²) **TYPOLOGY** Cultural, Exhibition
PHOTOGRAPHY Imagen Subliminal

Our installation in Casa Batlló in Barcelona is a tribute to Antoni Gaudí's genius use of light. However, where Gaudí layered color through the eight-story central atrium to modulate natural light, we achieved a similar effect through aluminum chain links.

We distilled the essence of Gaudi's vision into a poetic abstraction of light and reimagined the enclosed eight-story emergency stairwell as an ethereal, everchanging spectral experience. Sheathed in a series of suspended, cascading, curving aluminum chain screens, the stairwell captures artificial light and references the organic forms inside Casa Batlló.

The textural aluminum curtains shift subtly in tone, from bright silver at the rooftop to near black when they reach the depths of the basement, echoing the way daylight filters through the atrium. Within this otherwise dark space, lighting developed by designer Mario Nanni of Viabizzuno reflects off the metal links to enhance their shimmering quality.

The mesh screens are created with 102 miles (164 kilometers) of Kriskadecor aluminum chains. The individual chain-link strands are suspended from the variously inclined ceilings and surfaces underneath the stairs. By using only chains and erasing the presence of the walls, the staircase speaks only of light.

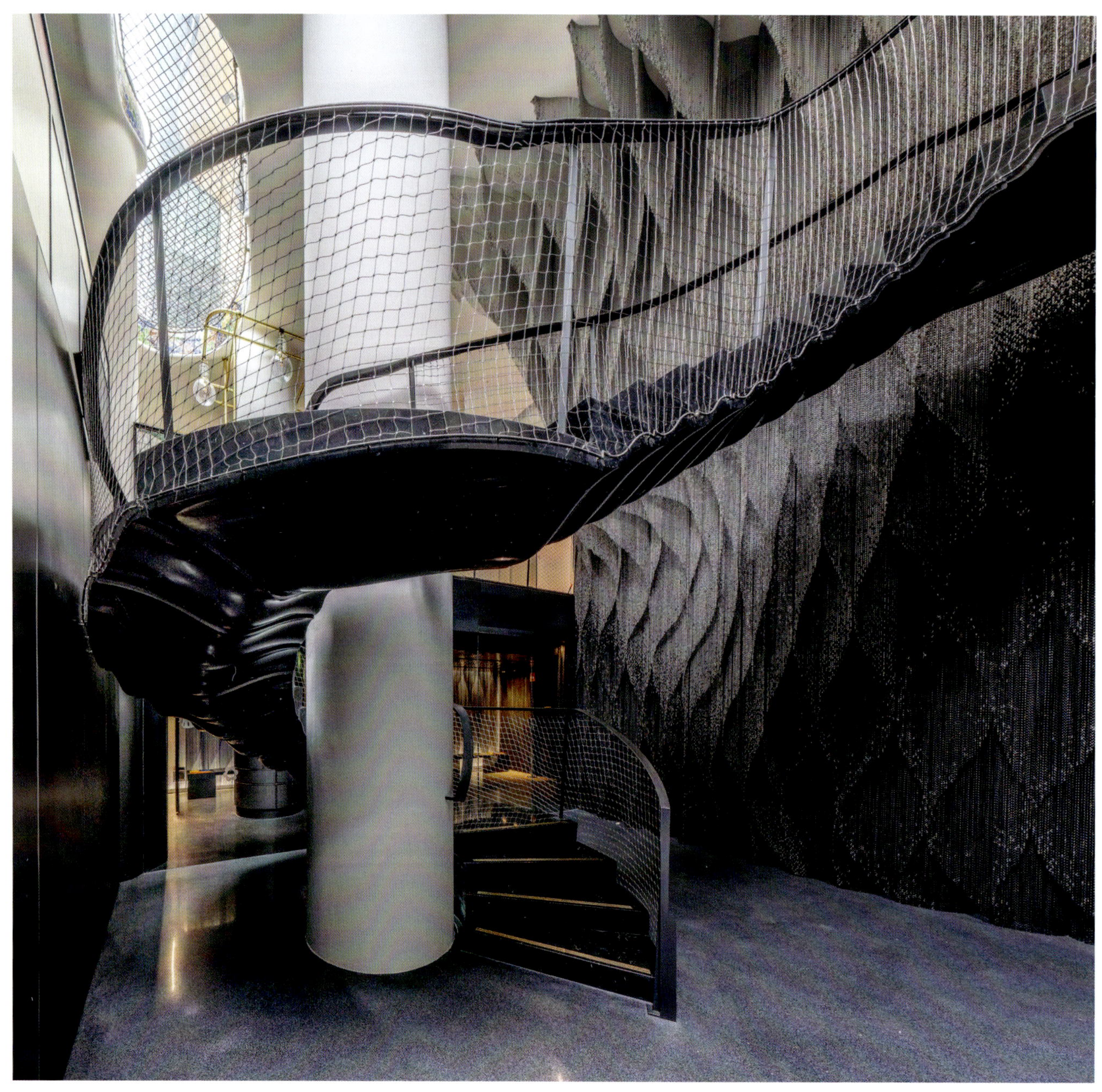

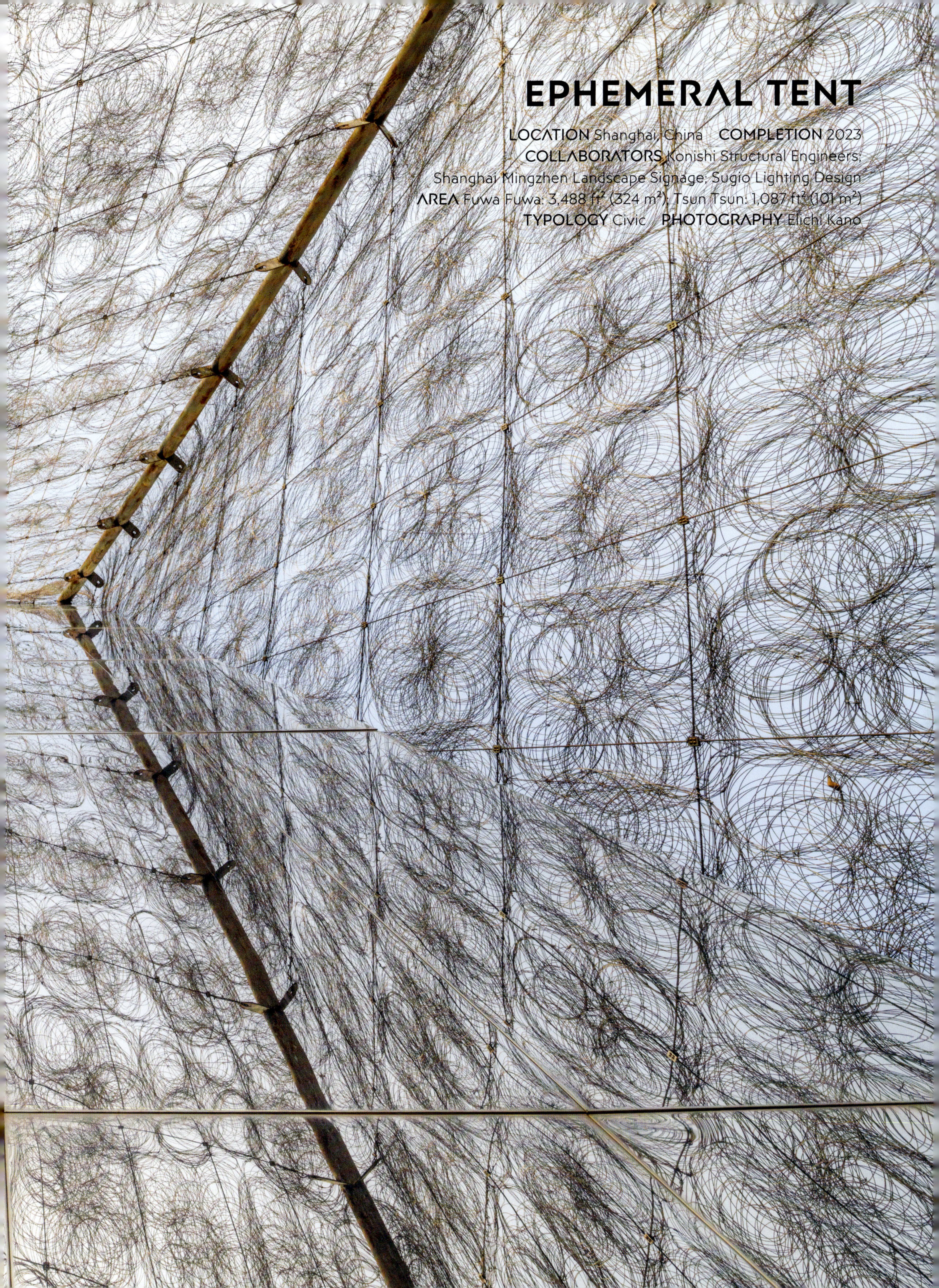

EPHEMERAL TENT

LOCATION Shanghai, China **COMPLETION** 2023
COLLABORATORS Konishi Structural Engineers; Shanghai Mingzhen Landscape Signage; Sugio Lighting Design
AREA Fuwa Fuwa: 3,488 ft^2 (324 m^2); Tsun Tsun: 1,087 ft^2 (101 m^2)
TYPOLOGY Civic **PHOTOGRAPHY** Eiichi Kano

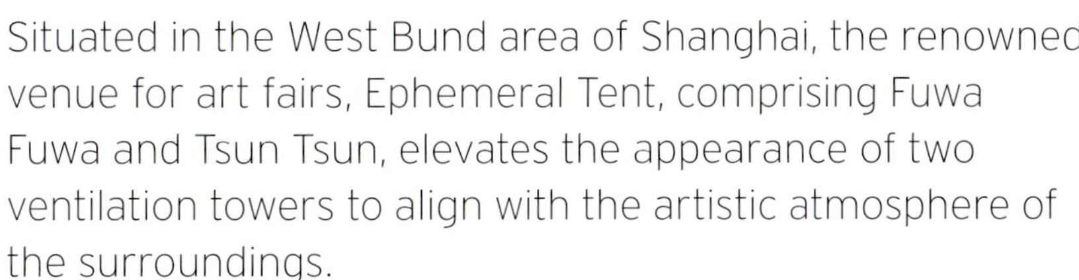

Situated in the West Bund area of Shanghai, the renowned venue for art fairs, Ephemeral Tent, comprising Fuwa Fuwa and Tsun Tsun, elevates the appearance of two ventilation towers to align with the artistic atmosphere of the surroundings.

Fuwa Fuwa—meaning 'fluffy fluffy'—is a tent-like form suspended from a 59-foot-tall (18-meter-tall) ventilation tower. Made with soft and lightweight 0.08-inch-diameter (2-millimeter-diameter) aluminum wire manually wound into spirals on a base of stainless-steel cables, its texture conjures the sensation of drifting clouds, blurring the line between reality and unreality. Entering inside, the mirrored surfaces cladding the tower enhance the spatial depth, giving rise to a wondrous environment that evokes the feeling of being embraced by clouds.

Tsun Tsun—meaning 'pointy pointy'—wraps the other ventilation tower in aluminum louvers in the same way fabric would drape around it. These spiky L-shaped aluminum louvers, arranged at various angles, softly reflect light, blending the background walls and the ventilation tower into the sky.

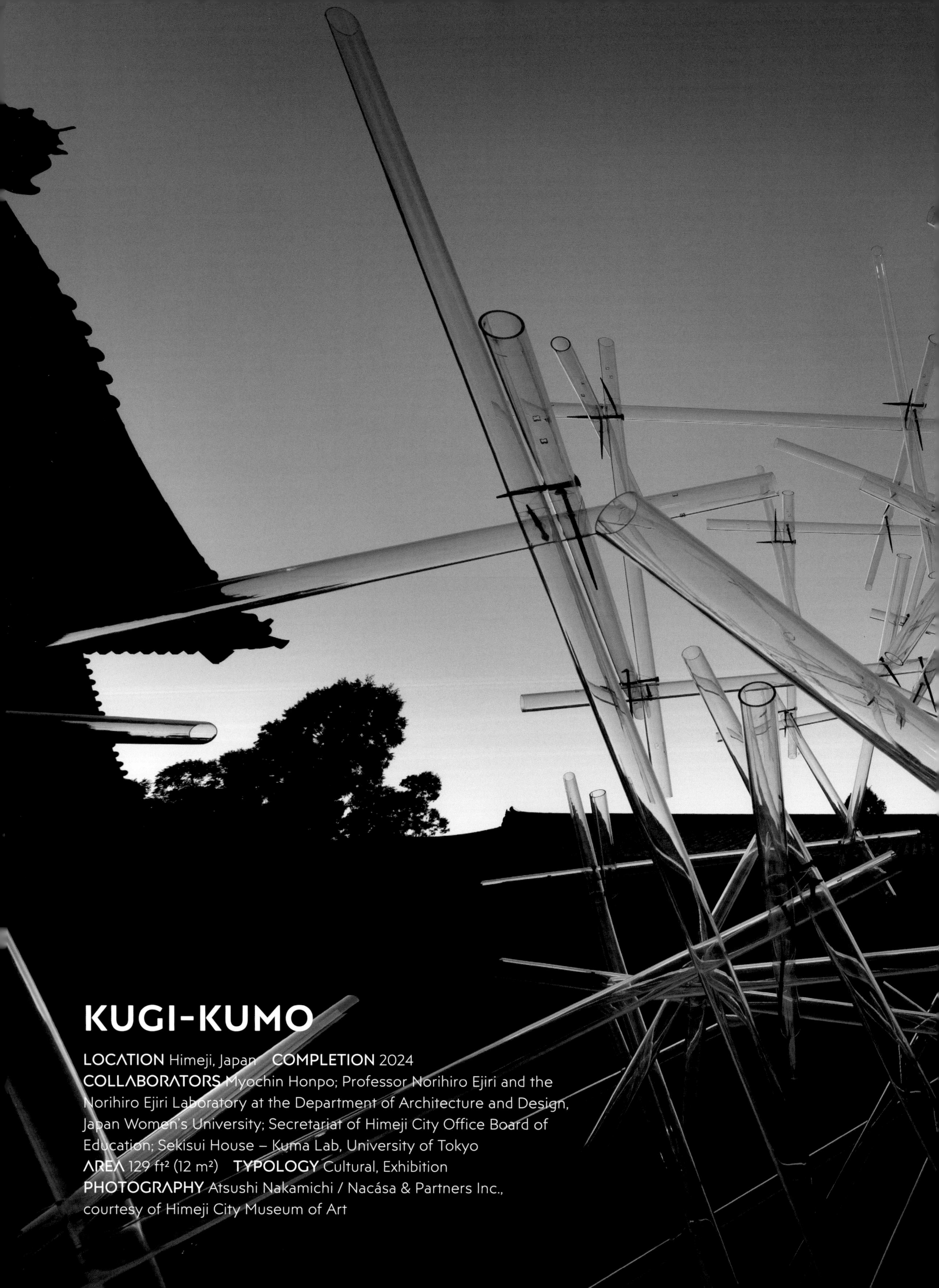

KUGI-KUMO

LOCATION Himeji, Japan **COMPLETION** 2024
COLLABORATORS Myochin Honpo; Professor Norihiro Ejiri and the Norihiro Ejiri Laboratory at the Department of Architecture and Design, Japan Women's University; Secretariat of Himeji City Office Board of Education; Sekisui House – Kuma Lab, University of Tokyo
AREA 129 ft² (12 m²) **TYPOLOGY** Cultural, Exhibition
PHOTOGRAPHY Atsushi Nakamichi / Nacása & Partners Inc., courtesy of Himeji City Museum of Art

Wakugi, traditional Japanese nails, differ from mass-produced Western nails. They are handcrafted one at a time and their square cross section (instead of round) provides a high level of adhesion to wood. Made with soft iron, they can be hammered into timber while avoiding the hard knots, making them well suited to wooden structures.

We used *wakugi* to create Kugi-Kumo ('cloud of nails') on the grounds of the ancient Engyoji Temple in Himeji. The traditional nails and technique have been passed down the generations in this city and famously used in the restoration of Himeji Castle.

Since these attractive-looking nails aren't normally visible in construction, due to being embedded in wood, we used them to connect transparent polycarbonate pipes. This shows off the beautiful shape of the nails and the technique, with the desire to revive and continue the tradition.

Digital fabrication was used to cut the holes in the polycarbonate pipes based on calculations made by structural engineer and professor Norihiro Ejiri. By integrating traditional craftsmanship and contemporary technology, Kugi-Kumo celebrates *wakugi*, with the nails appearing to disperse into the air like a cloud.

MUSHIZUKA

LOCATION Kamakura, Japan **COMPLETION** 2015
COLLABORATORS Ejiri Structural Engineers; Misumi Kensetsu; Syuhei Hasado
AREA 614 ft^2 (57 m^2) **TYPOLOGY** Monument
PHOTOGRAPHY Noboru Aoki / Shinchosha

It's a Japanese tradition to create various *zuka* ('burial mounds') to show respect for animals and objects at the end of their life. Mushizuka, located on the grounds of the Kencho-ji temple in Kamakura, is a transparent mound and monument for the repose of insects. It challenges the notion that monuments should be solid, usually tending to be built of stone or bronze.

The idea came from anatomist and insect collector Dr. Takeshi Yoro. He wanted to build a monument for the bugs he had been collecting as specimens to celebrate their life and contribution to his research. We created a monument that is almost unnoticeable, like the bugs Yoro wished to celebrate. It's named Mushizuka, as *mushi* means 'ignore' in Japanese.

The forty cages, like gigantic insect cages, are made with stainless-steel wire mesh and stacked in a spiral arrangement to express the insects gliding high in the sky. Traditional plasterwork (*sakan*) craftsman Syuhei Hasado sprayed the mesh with clay containing glass fiber and local earth. This unique materiality gives the cages a natural, organic appearance that feels soft and warm while retaining the transparency and clarity of the small, light, almost winged structure.

文具のやひこ堂
0423-93-6045
今井

WAKUNI SHOTEN

LOCATION Tokyo, Japan **COMPLETION** 2023
COLLABORATORS Okaniwa Kensetsu; Uchino Bankin Inc.
AREA 560 ft² (52 m²) **TYPOLOGY** Hospitality
PHOTOGRAPHY Kawasumi Kobayashi Kenji Photograph Office

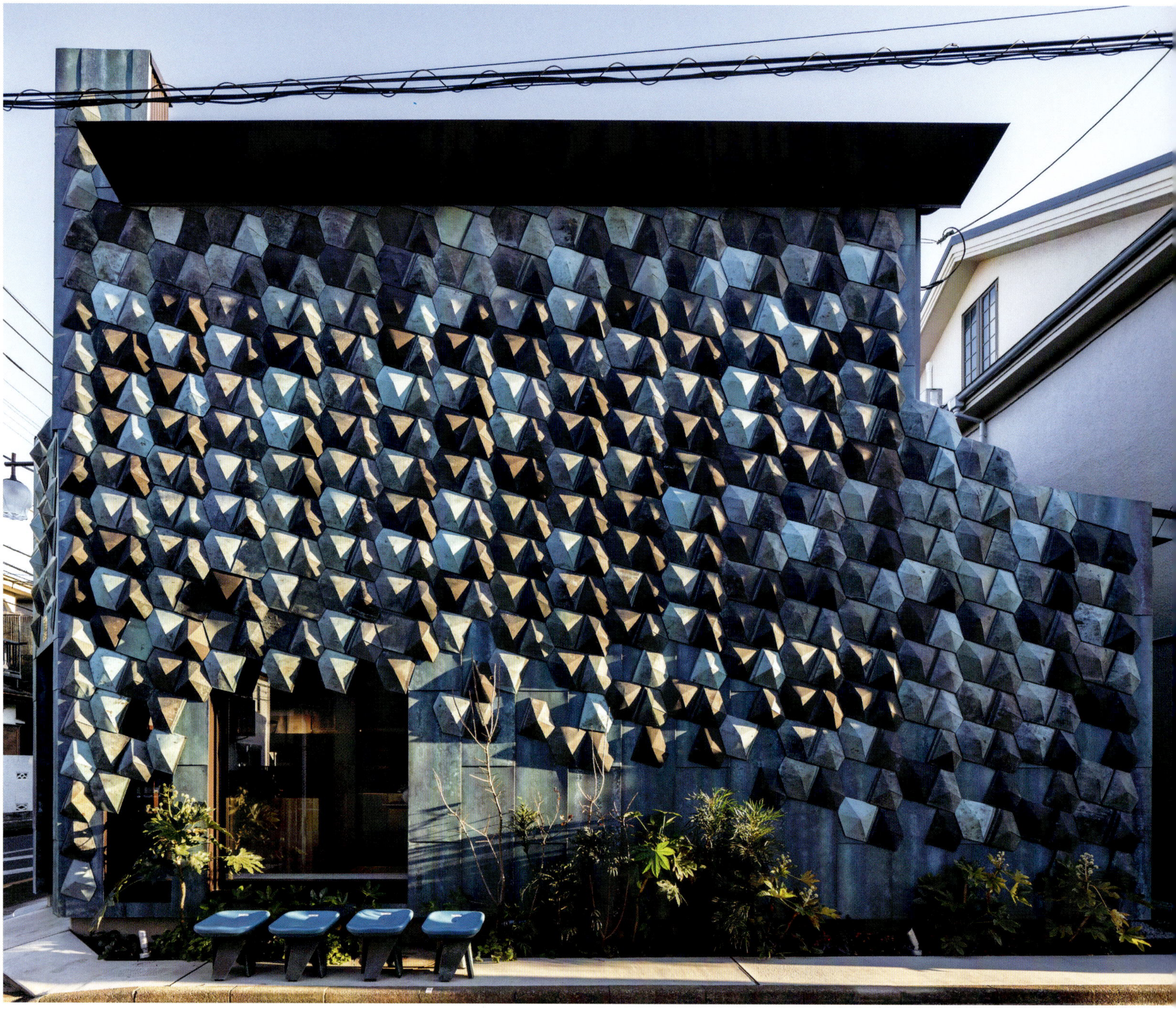

Wakuni Shoten showcases the skill of metalworking and celebrates the enduring spirit of Japanese craftsmanship. The café occupies a former tobacco store located on a shuttered street in the Aoba shopping district in Higashi-Murayama, Tokyo. Expressing a contemporary interpretation of tradition, we clad the exterior with 700 verdigris copper plates in an origami-like arrangement.

The copper plates were recycled from the roof of Hayatani Shrine in Hiroshima Prefecture. The owner of Wakuni Shoten and head of Uchino Bankin Inc., Tomokazu Uchino, along with his team, painstakingly reshaped the plates into pentagons. The result is a three-dimensional, textural, patterned façade that changes in color depending on how the sun hits it at different times of the day and season.

Like *kanban kenchiku* ('signboard architecture') that emerged after the 1923 Great Kantō Earthquake, Wakuni Shoten's façade doubles as an advertisement and showcase for what's inside. The black plaster walls of the interior provide a backdrop for metalwork furniture and fittings, including our Uzu lampshade sculpted to look like a whirlpool.

Echoing the theme of reuse, the outdoor chairs are crafted from salvaged seats of the former National Stadium, to which we added legs reminiscent of the Olympic cauldron.

文具のやひこ堂
0423-83-6045

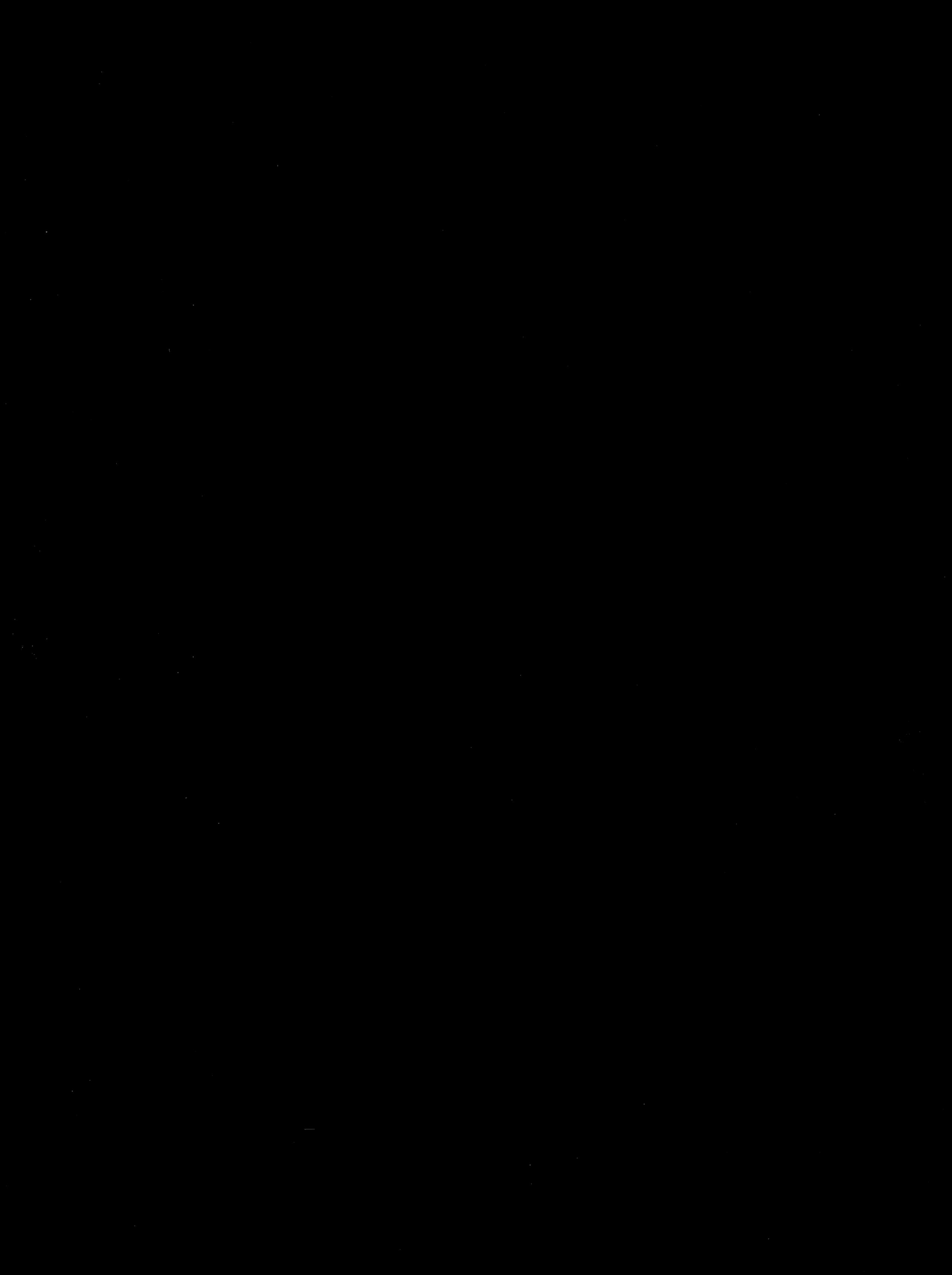

PAPER

PAPER SNAKE

LOCATION Anyang, South Korea **COMPLETION** 2005
COLLABORATORS Ejiri Structural Engineers; F8's; M-tec
AREA 323 ft² (30 m²) **TYPOLOGY** Civic, Cultural
PHOTOGRAPHY Kengo Kuma & Associates

Paper Snake is a public art project and resting space designed for Anyang, on the periphery of Seoul. Located on a beautiful forest hillside, Paper Snake occupies a privileged position where the path meets the pine trees, and the folded forms frame the idyllic scenery with views down the valley to the river.

We designed the folded platform to create and envelope space, and to react and respond to the surrounding nature. No side is parallel or symmetrical to another, forming an organic, winding snake-like structure that sits harmoniously in its forest setting.

To achieve the flexible, durable pavilion, we worked with the engineers to invent a structural panel. Made with a 1.57-inch-thick (40-millimeter-thick) paper honeycomb core compressed by two fiberglass reinforced plastic (FRP) sheets, the panel is extremely lightweight, while also being remarkably strong, and recyclable.

As the light and shadows gently pass through and across the porous material, its translucent and luminous quality registers the surrounding conditions. By translating the natural phenomenon directly on to the structure, Paper Snake becomes a sensitive receiver of the site and a calming, tranquil environment for visitors.

IRORI & PAPER COCOON

LOCATION Milan, Italy **COMPLETION** 2015
COLLABORATORS Ejiri Structural Engineers; Kitchenhouse; Time & Style; TJM Design; Viabizzuno **AREA** 700 ft² (65 m²) **TYPOLOGY** Cultural, Exhibition
PHOTOGRAPHY Takumi Ota

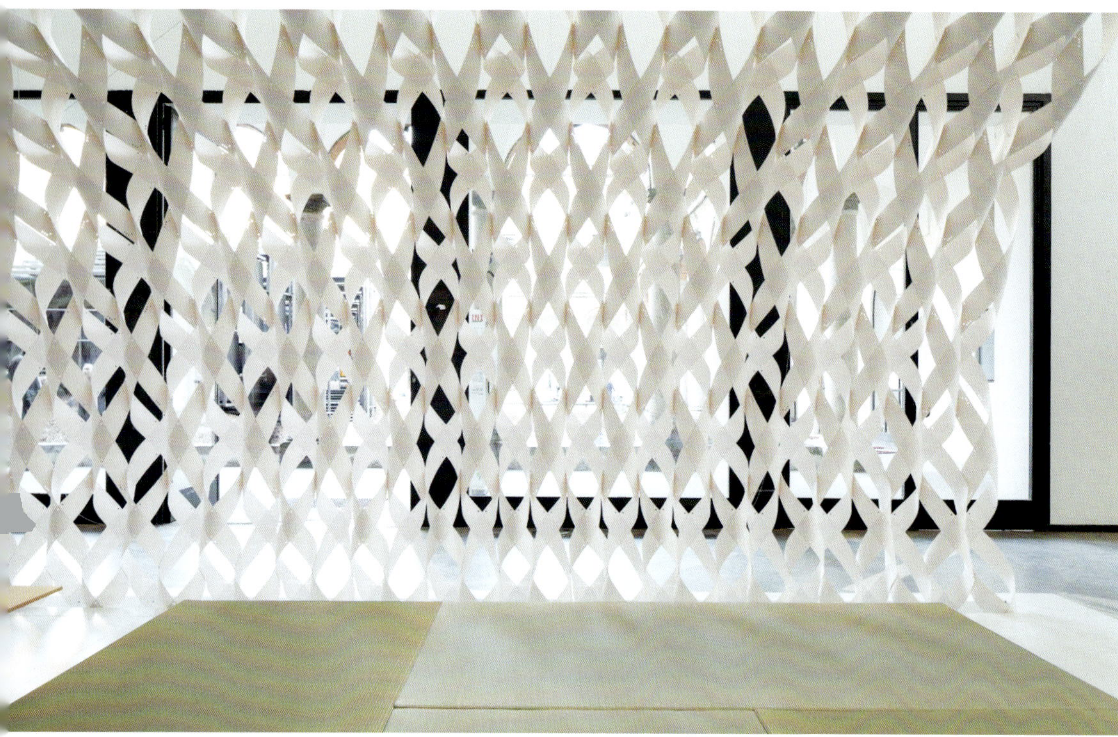

We designed Irori & Paper Cocoon for the Energy for Creativity program organized by Interni at Salon del Mobile 2015. The contemporary kitchen space represents a new way of living. It is centered around fire, which is deeply ingrained in human tradition, and set within a cocoon, a symbol for a new phase of life or growth.

The kitchen is like a freehand landscape that can expand and contract with life. The modular bamboo-board and steel-pipe components can be configured into tables, benches, and shelves of varying scales and sizes. Instead of a stove, a traditional sunken hearth—known as *irori* in Japanese—is a separate yet connected living space that becomes the heart of the kitchen and the household.

Enclosing the kitchen is a light, translucent, and protective cocoon. Made with 0.04-inch-thick (1-millimeter-thick) vulcanized paper, it has greater rigidity than normal paper, while maintaining a level of softness. The supple material has been gently twisted, woven, and stretched to form the arched structure.

TEXTILE

CERAMIC YIN YANG

LOCATION Milan, Italy **COMPLETION** 2010
COLLABORATORS Amaike Textile Industry; Casalgrande Padana; Viabizzuno
TYPOLOGY Cultural, Exhibition **PHOTOGRAPHY** Kengo Kuma & Associates

For the Interni Think Tank at Fuorisalone during the Salone del Mobile 2010, we installed a 'wall' of organza curtain diagonally dividing the Bagni delle Donne courtyard, one of four courtyards in Cortile dei Bagni within the University of Milan. Recognizing the cruciality of sustainable design, the exhibition proposed reflections on ways in which the productive system behind design can contribute to new solutions and outcomes, and how historical sites can be used in innovative ways.

Our installation represented an abstraction of Casalgrande Ceramic Cloud that we designed for Casalgrande Padana in Reggio Emilia. The monumental wall experimented with anti-volume and anti-matter, and dynamic principles such as time, movement, and sequential perception.

These concepts become more extreme in the exhibition in Milan. The organza curtain divided the courtyard into two gardens with ceramic pieces to one side, and siliceous stones to the other, highlighting the similarities and contrasts as a metaphor for yin and yang. During the day, the light, semi-transparent wall simultaneously veiled and unveiled the courtyard. At night, it was transformed into a screen with projections of solids and voids and plays of light and shadow. In an accelerated way, the projection showed the passing of time across a full day.

Along the loggia, a sequence of installations placed in rooms facing the courtyard connected Ceramic Yin Yang with Ceramic Cloud through a series of videos and live cams.

DESIGN SUPER MARKET
INTERNI THINK TANK
Kengo Kuma
CASALGRANDE PADANA
Thanks to:
SHARP, VIABIZZUNO
INTERNI THINK TANK
Rinascente
INTERNI
MONDADORI

CASA UMBRELLA

LOCATION Milan, Italy **COMPLETION** 2008
AREA 161 ft² (15 m²) **TYPOLOGY** Cultural, Exhibition
PHOTOGRAPHY Yoshie Nishikawa

Casa Umbrella is literally a pop-up shelter, in which every element of the design adapts the components of a common umbrella. We designed Casa Umbrella for an exhibition of temporary housing prototypes at *Casa per Tutti (Housing for All)* at the Milan Triennial. Set forth as a proposal for temporary emergency housing, our prototype was based on using materials easily found at supermarkets, and it had to be lightweight, easy to carry, and waterproof.

We selected the everyday umbrella and developed a light, foldable version made with Tyvek, an innovative polyethylene non-woven fabric that offers outstanding quality in water proofing, moisture proofing, and is easy to sew.

The umbrellas are arranged into a three-dimensional structure based on the mechanics of an umbrella, and reminiscent of Buckminster Fuller's geodesic dome. Each triangle on a regular icosahedron is replaced by an umbrella, and a triangle created by the bones of each umbrella is utilized as the truss structure, visible inside the pavilion. Zippers (from diving suits) connect the umbrellas along their outer edges. This means a new space can be produced in an open space by simply opening the umbrella and fastening the zipper.

The size and number of the umbrellas is based on the intended spaces to be created. A few umbrellas can produce a small roof or a partition, while fifteen umbrellas can create a pavilion. On a rainy day, the pavilion becomes a rain shelter. On a fine day, it becomes a small arbor by opening a zipper to bring in a natural light and a gentle breeze. During a disaster, if every person has an umbrella, then groups of people can build temporary shelters together.

NAMAKO

LOCATION Canberra, Australia **COMPLETION** 2018
COLLABORATORS Ejiri Structural Engineers; University of Canberra; University of Tokyo
AREA 108 ft² (10 m²) **TYPOLOGY** Cultural, Exhibition
PHOTOGRAPHY Kengo Kuma Laboratory; University of Canberra; University of Tokyo

Seeing architecture as fundamentally a process of weaving, our practice not only engages in the weaving of things, but also the weaving of techniques, materials, ideas, spaces, people, and fields outside of architecture.

Namako—the inaugural, ephemeral architecture project that launched Design Canberra Festival 2018—conceptually and physically expresses our interest in investigating the possibilities of different types of weaving. We designed the installation, set on Aspen Island on Lake Burley Griffin, to encourage interaction between it, visitors, and the surrounding natural environment.

The 9.8-foot-high (3-meter-high) and 39.3-foot-wide (12-meter-wide) tubular structure is made with bio-acrylic rods, eucalyptus dowels, and a mesh of zip ties. Produced through a reckless weaving process, Namako evokes the softness, transparency, texture, and form of the sea cucumber—*namako* in Japanese. These unique characteristics encouraged visitors' interaction with the pavilion and fostered its rich relationship to the surrounding context.

The project also celebrated Canberra's 25th anniversary with its sister city, Nara, in Japan. The construction was carried out by students at the University of Canberra, who had previously participated in the collaborative process of weaving the prototype with students from the University of Tokyo in a faculty-led program to Japan.

Hello, I am NAMAKO.
I like to be touched
but I don't like to be
climbed.

KXK (KRUG X KUMA = ∞)

LOCATION Tokyo, Japan **COMPLETION** 2003
COLLABORATORS Nomura Company; Oak Strucutural Design **AREA** 75 ft² (7 m²)
TYPOLOGY Cultural, Exhibition **PHOTOGRAPHY** Color Kinetics Japan

It has always been my dream that architecture can be living, like an animal, rather than stationary and static, with a rigid, invariable shape. We designed this living, ever-moving dome for an event hosted by French champagne maker Krug at the Hara Museum of Contemporary Art in Minato.

We made the dome with a shape-memory alloy that grows or shrinks depending on the ambient temperature. The extremely soft EVA (ethylene-vinyl acetate) membrane is a 0.08-inch-diameter (2-millimeter-diameter) corded resin supported by a 0.08-inch-diameter (2-millimeter-diameter) shape-memory alloy frame. More of an assimilated membrane than a frame, it is intended to neutralize the dichotomy of membrane versus frame.

As the shape-memory alloy undergoes a phase transformation, changing its shape in response to shifts in temperature, the dome moves, becoming more biological than architectural. Cooling eliminates the rigidity of the alloy, making it possible to fold the dome to fit into a small container and transport it around the world.

KITHUL-AMI

LOCATION Bentota, Sri Lanka **COMPLETION** 2020
AREA 431 ft² (40 m²) **TYPOLOGY** Cultural, Exhibition
PHOTOGRAPHY Kengo Kuma & Associates

Kithul-Ami is a pavilion designed for the centenary celebration of Sri Lankan architect Geoffery Bawa's birth. Located on Lunuganga Estate, Bawa's former country house, the pavilion offers a moment of repose and reflection and can also be used for tea ceremonies and similar gatherings.

Our design draws inspiration from the soft, luminous curves of the steel furniture Bawa designed for Heritance Kandalama Hotel, and from the local kithul craft, in which strands of the kithul flower (*Caryota urens*) are dried and woven into household objects. We worked with local metalsmith Indika Kumarasingha and weaver Disna Shiromali, and their teams, to create the pavilion using steel mesh and kithul. Our goal was to try and capture the softness of Bawa's architecture and showcase that his individuality is rooted in the nature and culture of Sri Lanka.

Avoiding sharpness and rectilinearity, the pavilion is a continuous 248-foot-long (75.6-meter-long) ribbon that gently twists and turns, touching the earth lightly. We achieved the fluid and flexible single-curved surface using physics-simulation software.

Like Bawa's architecture, Kithul-Ami is in harmony with nature, casting beautiful shadows and embracing those within it. The undulating form also evokes a wave, an important symbol in Sri Lankan and Japanese cultures, as both countries have a long history with ocean.

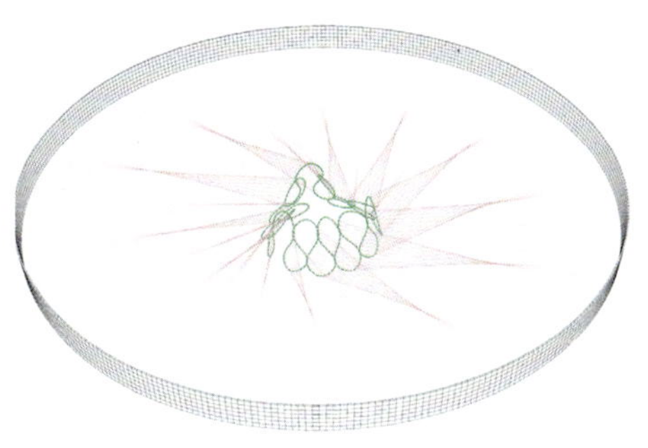

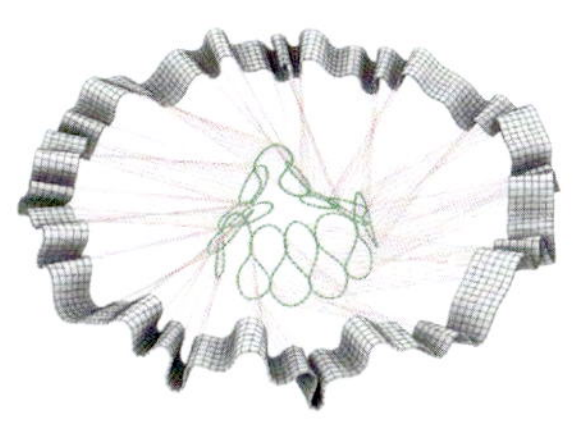

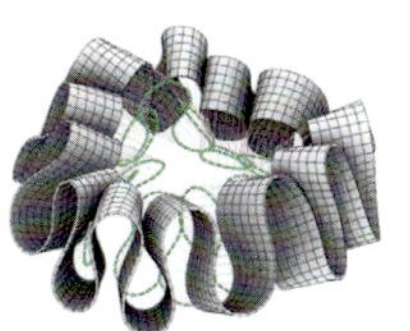

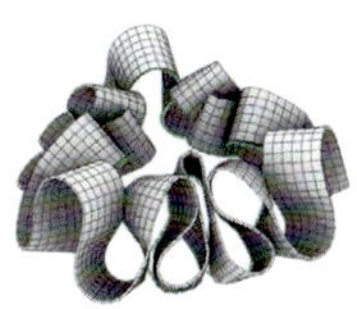

DIAGRAM

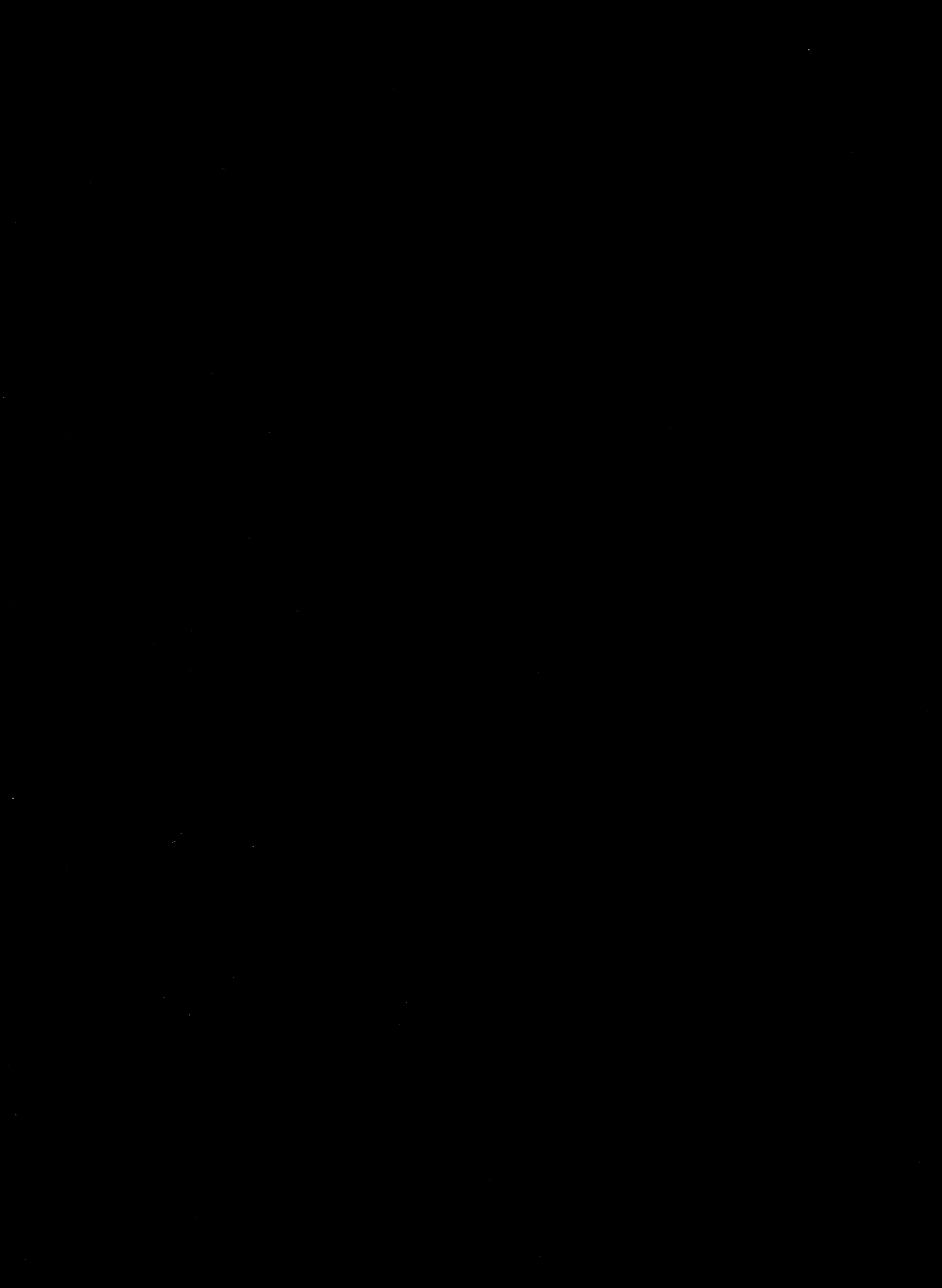

STONE

STONE FOREST

LOCATION Milan, Italy **COMPLETION** 2014
COLLABORATORS Ejiri Structural Engineers; Salvatori; Viabizzuno
AREA 387 ft² (36 m²) **TYPOLOGY** Cultural, Exhibition
PHOTOGRAPHY Kengo Kuma & Associates

Interested in achieving lightness through natural materials, I wanted to create the illusion or paradox of lightness by using heavy stone.

Our design of the Stone Forest for the Salone del Mobile 2014 is based on the ancient woodworking technique *jigoku-gumi*, a precise joint system used to make grids in traditional Japanese architecture. Individual components are joined without nails or glue; two layers overlap each other and are secured systematically with a third layer, until the entire lattice-like structure acts as a cohesive, self-supporting frame.

We used Bianco Carrara stone for its pure aesthetic and structural strength, while still retaining the essential lightness of the traditional wood structure. The upright and diagonal stone struts are interlocked and fixed with a simple wooden dowel, acting as a pin holding the two stone slats together.

The construction technique builds layer upon layer to create a three-dimensional impression, achieving lightness through a natural material.

CAVE OF LIGHT AND SHADOW

LOCATION Suzhou, China **COMPLETION** 2023
COLLABORATORS Ejiri Structural Engineers **AREA** 1,938 ft² (180 m²)
TYPOLOGY Monument **PHOTOGRAPHY** Fangfang Tian

Taihu stone, the symbol of nature in Suzhou, was the theme for a porous and transparent monument we designed for the front courtyard of the Suzhou Museum.

Taihu is a water-eroded limestone known for its infinite holes and unique and complex shapes. We imitated the character of the stone by using aluminum casting technology and strong, lightweight, porous aluminum.

The perforated and textured panels are in a perpendicular arrangement and fused together to create a monument designed to be experienced.

While ordinary monuments exist as a type of object that people experience from the outside, we realized a monument that people experience by passing through the inside. Sunlight also passes between the panels and filters through the holes, casting gentle and intricate shadows and reflections on the water surface.

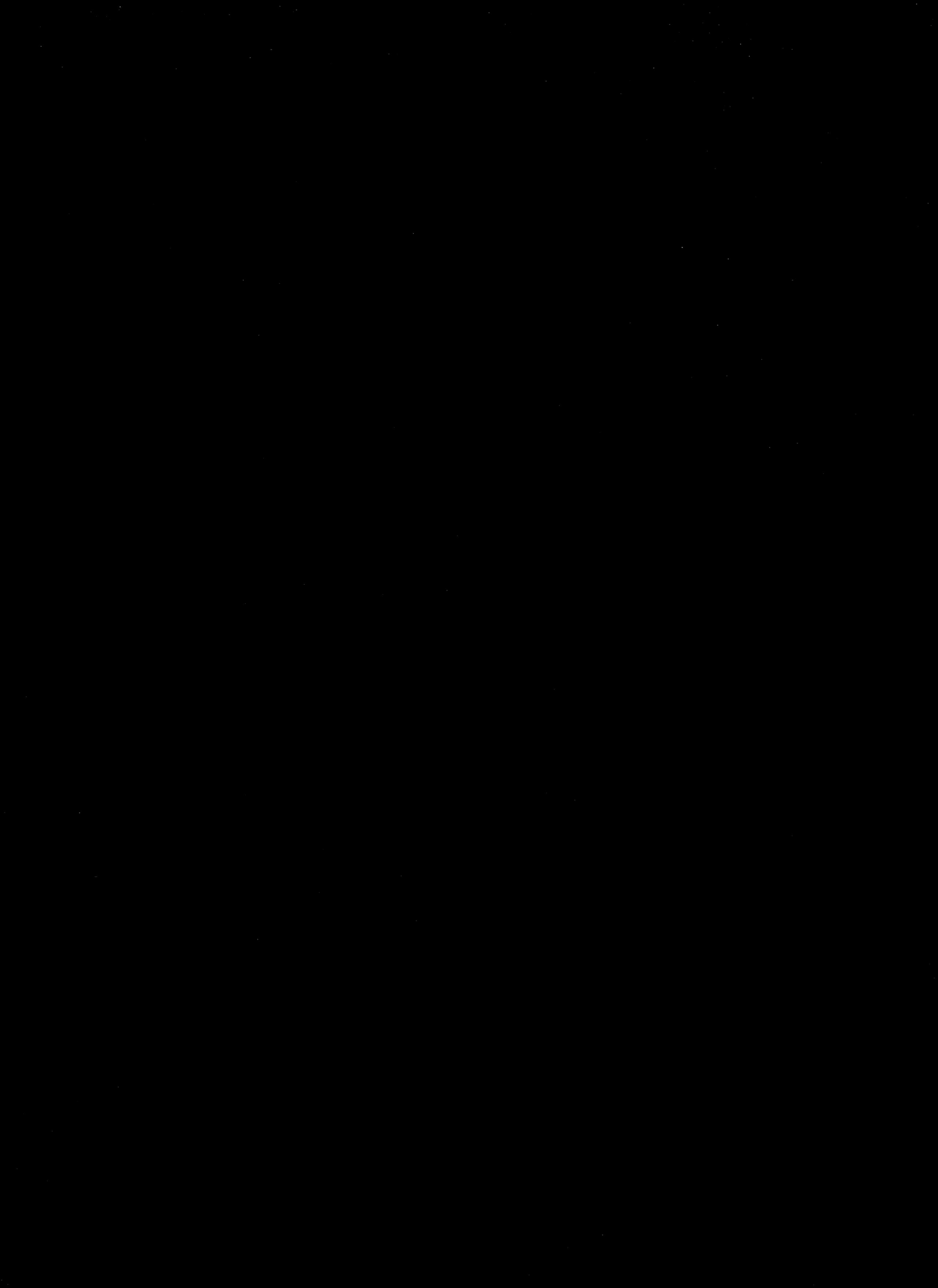

APPENDIX

INDEX OF PROJECTS

AUSTRALIA

Botanical Pavilion 48-53
Namako 226-35

CHINA

Bamboo Flow 134-39
Bamboo Passage 128-33
Cave of Light and Shadow 254-59
Ephemeral Tent 164-73

FRANCE

Komorebi 40-47
Yure 22-27

ITALY

Casa Umbrella 216-25
Ceramic Yin Yang 210-15
Cidori 28-33
Domino 3.0 12-17
Irori & Paper Cocoon 200-207
Kodama 54-61
Stone Forest 248-53

JAPAN

CLT Park Harumi 70-77
Kugi-Kumo 174-79
Kusugibashi 108-15
KXK (Krug x Kuma = ∞) 236-39
Mushizuka 180-85
Nakahashi 98-107
One Health Carbon Gate 142-47
Sana Mane Sazae Sauna 88-97
Uro-co 82-87
Wakuni Shoten 186-91

MEXICO

Casa Wabi Coop 62-69

POLAND

The Cloud 18-21

SINGAPORE

Wooden Haze 78-81

SOUTH KOREA

Nangchang-Nangchang 118-21
Neowa Dome 34-39
Paper Snake 194-99

SPAIN

Casa Batlló Stairs 152-63

SRI LANKA

Kithul-Ami 240-45

SWITZERLAND

Owan 148-51

UNITED KINGDOM

Sensing Spaces 122-27

BIOGRAPHY

Kengo Kuma was born in 1954. He decided at a young age to pursue architecture, having been inspired by Kenzo Tange's Yoyogi National Gymnasium, built for the 1964 Tokyo Olympics. He studied architecture at the University of Tokyo and received his master's degree in 1979.

In 1990, he established Kengo Kuma & Associates (KKAA). Headquartered in Tokyo, the firm also has offices in Paris, Beijing, Shanghai, and Seoul, and Kengo Kuma & Associates projects are currently underway in more than fifty countries.

Kengo Kuma proposes architecture that opens new relationships between nature, technology, and human beings. He is currently a university professor and professor emeritus at the University of Tokyo, and a member of the Japan Art Academy after teaching at Keio University and the University of Tokyo.

AWARDS AND RECOGNITION

A selection of awards and recognition for Kengo Kuma and Kengo Kuma & Associates.

1997 First Place, Architectural Institute of Japan Award: Noh Stage in the Forest

American Institute of Architects (AIA) DuPont Benedictus Award: Water / Glass

2001 Togo Murano Award and Architectural Institute Award: Nakagawa-machi Bato Hiroshige Museum of Art

International Stone Architecture Award: Stone Museum

2002 Spirit of Nature Wood Architecture Award, Finland

2008 Energy Performance + Architecture Award, France

Bobat Wood Award: Sakenohana

Bois Magazine International Award for Wood Architecture, France

2009 Royal Institute of British Architects (RIBA) International Fellowship, United Kingdom

Decoration L'Ordre des Arts et des Lettres, France

2010 Mainichi Art Award: Nezu Museum

2011 American Institute of Architects (AIA) Honorary Fellowship, United States

The Minister of Education, Culture, Sports, Science and Technology's Art Encouragement Prize: Yusuhara Wooden Bridge Museum

2015 ELLE DECO International Design Awards, Best in Kitchens nominated by Japan Edition: Irori & Paper Cocoon

2016 Global Award for Sustainable Architecture, France

First Prize, National Award of France; First Prize, Regional Award of Rhone-Alpes; and Winner of Public Choice Award for Wood Construction: Mont-Blanc Base Camp

Public Buildings Award of Excellence for Governmental Building: City Hall Plaza Aore Nagaoka

2017 Product Design of the Year, European Product Design Award for Home Interior Products: Cidori

2018 Interior Design Hall of Fame, United States

Architectural Institute of Japan (AIJ) Award in Education

Wallpaper* Design Awards for Best Façade: V&A Dundee

2019 Asian Cultural Council John D. Rockefeller 3rd Award, United States

Medal with Purple Ribbon, Japan

Military Order of Savoy (Cavaliere di Gran Croce; Grand Cross of the Equestrian Order), Italy

2020 Japan Wood Design Award of Excellence, Director General of Forestry Agency Prize: CLT Park Harumi

Japan Institute of Design Promotion Good Design Award: CLT Park Harumi

2021 Time100: The Most Influential People of 2021, United States

2022 Popular Choice Winner and Jury Winner, Architizer A+ Awards for Architecture + Art: Botanical Pavilion

2024 DFA Lifetime Achievement Award, Hong Kong

IFI Prize, United States

ORIS Keraterm Award, Croatia

PULSE Awards Jan Kaplicky Award, Czech Republic

Imperial Prize and Japan Art Academy Prize: V&A Dundee

Order of Merit of the Italian Republic, Italy

2025 38th Louis I. Kahn Award, United States

EXHIBITIONS

A selection of solo and group exhibitions for Kengo Kuma and Kengo Kuma & Associates.

1992 *Tokyo Columns* / M2, Setagaya, Tokyo, Japan

1993 *City of Labyrinth* / Sezon Museum of Art, Toshimaku, Tokyo / Tsukashin Hall, Amagasaki, Hyogo, Japan

1995 *Velocity of Transmission* / Gallery MA, Minato, Tokyo, Japan

1997 *Virtual Architecture* / The University Museum, University of Tokyo, Bunkyo, Tokyo, Japan

2001 *Japanese Avant-Garde* / Reality Projection, 16 Young Japanese Architects / RIBA, London, United Kingdom

2004 *HAPTIC,* Takeo Paper Show 2004 / Spiral, Minato, Tokyo, Japan

New Trends of Architecture in Europe and Asia-Pacific 2004-2005 / Lille, France

Kengo Kuma: Defeated Architecture / Matsuya Ginza, Chuo, Tokyo, Japan

Niwa; Where the Particle Response / Hotel New Otani Garden Court, Chiyoda, Tokyo, Japan

3_2_1_New Architecture in Japan and Poland / Manggha Museum of Japanese Art and Technology, Kraków, Poland

Archilab: New Experiments in Architecture, Art and the City, 1950-2005 / Mori Art Museum, Minato, Tokyo, Japan

2005 *Kengo Kuma: The Architecture Between Tradition and Innovation* / Siracusa / Milan / Naples, Italy; Stockholm, Sweden

Extreme Eurasia / Spiral, Minato, Tokyo, Japan

Kuma Mock-Ups / GA Gallery, Shibuya, Tokyo, Japan

2006 *GA International 2006* / GA Gallery, Shibuya, Tokyo, Japan

2007 *100 years of Mondadori Milano Capitale del Design Decode Elements* / Castello Sforzesco, Milan, Italy

Two Carps: Water/Land – Village/Urban – Phenomenology, Barbara Cappochin International Biennal Architecture / Palazzo dela Ragione, Padova, Italy

2008 *MOMA Home Delivery Fabricating the Modern Dwelling* / New York, United States

Material Immaterial / I-Space, Chicago, United States

2012 *Hojo-an after 800 Years* / Kyoto, Japan

2016 *House Vision 2016* / Rinkai Fukutoshin J Area, Aomi, Koto-ku, Tokyo, Japan

Book-Architecture Exhibition, Korea-China-Japan Locus Design Forum / Dongdaemun Design Plaza, Seoul, South Korea

2017 *Kengo Kuma: Eterno Efêmero* / Japan House, São Paulo, Brazil

Japan Unlayered / Fairmont Pacific Rim, Vancouver, Canada

Small Architecture / Asakusa Culture Tourist Information Center, Tokyo, Japan

2018 *Kengo Kuma: A Lab for Materials* / Tokyo, Japan; Shanghai, China

Exhibition of Architecture Models by 3D Printer / Tokyu Hands Shibuya, Tokyo, Japan

2019 *Insects: Models for Design* / 21_21 Design Sight, Tokyo, Japan

2020 *Secret Source of Inspiration: Designers' Hidden Sketches and Mockups* / 21_21 Design Sight, Tokyo, Japan

2021 *Kuma Kengo: Five Purr-Fect Points for a New Public Space* / The National Museum of Modern Art, Tokyo, Japan

2022 *Architectural Model: Historical Transition as a Medium of Architecture* / WHAT MUSEUM, Tokyo, Japan

Architecture for the Five Senses / Touring exhibition, China

Architecture / Sculpture for Itami City Hall: Kengo Kuma, Atsuhiko Misawa and Koji Tanada / Itami City Museum of Art, History and Culture, Itami, Japan

2024 *Kengo Kuma Exhibition* / Tokimori Gallery, Tokyo, Japan

Kenzo Tange and Kengo Kuma – Architects of the Tokyo Games / Japan Cultural Institute, Paris, France

Kengo Kuma and Portugal Architectural Dialogues / Hillside Forum, Daikanyama, Shibuya, Tokyo, Japan

The 80th Imperial Prize and the Japan Art Academy Prize Winners Exhibition / Japan Art Academy Headquarters, Tokyo, Japan

Kuma Sanpo – Kengo Kuma's Architecture and Sakai Town / S-Gallery, Sakai Town, Ibaraki, Japan

Kengo Kuma: Landscape Architecture – Hills, Mountains, Forests, Caves / Karuizawa New Art Museum, Karuizawa, Japan

Kenzo Tange and Kengo Kuma: Two National Stadiums / Design Gallery 1953, Matsuya Ginza, Tokyo, Japan

MONOGRAPHS AND PUBLICATIONS

A selection of monographs and publications by Kengo Kuma and other authors and publishers, as named.

1990 *Kengo Kuma: 10 Houses*, Toso Publishing, Tokyo, 1986 [paperback edition], Chikuma Publishing

1994 *Kengo Kuma: Introduction to Architecture-History and Ideology*, Chikuma Publishing, Tokyo, Japan

Kengo Kuma: Catastrophe of Architectural Desire, Shin'yosha, Tokyo, Japan

1995 *Kengo Kuma: Beyond the Architectural Crisis*, TOTO Publishing, Tokyo, Japan

1997 *Kengo Kuma: Digital Gardening*, Special issue of *Space Design*, Kajima Publishing, Tokyo, Japan

1999 *Kengo Kuma: Geometries of Nature*, L'Arca Edizioni, Milan, Italy

2000 *Kengo Kuma: The Japan Architect 38*, Shinkentiku-sha, Tokyo, Japan

Kengo Kuma: Anti-Object, Chikuma Publishing, Tokyo, Japan

2004 *Kengo Kuma: Materials, Structures, Details*, Shokokusha, Tokyo, Japan / Birkuhauser, Basel, Switzerland

Kengo Kuma: Defeated Architecture, Iwanami Shoten, Tokyo, Japan

2005 Botond Bognar, *Kengo Kuma: Selected Works*, Princeton Architectural Press, New York, United States

Luigi Alini, *Kengo Kuma: Opere e Progetti*, Mondadori Electa, Milan, Italy

GA, *GA Architect* 19: Kengo Kuma, A.D.A. Edita Tokyo, Tokyo, Japan

2006 *Kengo Kuma*, Edil Stampa, Rome, Italy

Luigi Alini, *Kengo Kuma: Works and Projects*, Mondadori Electa, Milan, Italy

2007 *Kengo Kuma*, C3, Seoul, South Korea

Marco Casamonti, *Kengo Kuma*, Motta Architettura, Milan, Italy

Kengo Kuma: Lecture and Dialogue, INAX Publishing, Tokyo, Japan

2008 *Build Built: The Exhibition of Kengo Kuma in China*, ZHUE Design Space, China Museum, Beijing, China

Volker Fischer and Ulrich Schneider, *Kengo Kuma: Breathing Architecture*, Birkhauser, Basel, Switzerland

Luigi Alini, *Kengo Kuma: Liticità Contemporanee. Da Stone Museum a Stone Pavilion*, Libria, Melfi, Italy

Kengo Kuma and Yumi Kiyono, *Shin Toshi-ron Tokyo [A New Debate on Cities]*, Shueisha Publishing, Tokyo, Japan

Kengo Kuma: A Natural Architecture, Iwanami Shoten, Tokyo, Japan

2009 GA, *Kengo Kuma: Recent Project*, A.D.A. Edita Tokyo, Tokyo, Japan

Studies in Organic, Toto Publishing, Tokyo, Japan

Botond Bognar, *Material Immaterial*, Princeton Architectural Press, New York, United States

2010 *NA Architect Series 02: Kengo Kuma*, Nikkei Business Publications, Tokyo, Japan

2012 *Maestri dell'Architettura e del Design: Kengo Kuma and Associates*, Hachette Fascicoli, Milan, Italy

GA, *Kengo Kuma 2006–2012*, A.D.A. Edita Tokyo, Tokyo, Japan

Kenneth Frampton, *Kengo Kuma: Complete Works*, Thames & Hudson, London, United Kingdom

2014 *Small Architecture / Natural Architecture* (translated by Alfred Birnbaum), Architectural Association, London, United Kingdom

AV Monographs 167–168, *Kengo Kuma 2000–2014*, Arquitectura Viva, Madrid, Spain

2015 *Kengo Kuma: Onomatopoeia Architecture*, X-Knowledge, Tokyo, Japan

2019 *Architecture of Defeat*, Routledge, London, United Kingdom

2020 *Ten Men Sen [Point Line Plane]*, Iwanami Shoten, Tokyo, Japan

Tokyo, Kadokawa, Tokyo, Japan

GA, *Kengo Kuma 2013–2020*, A.D.A. Edita Tokyo, Tokyo, Japan

AV Monographs 218–219, *Kengo Kuma 2014–2019*, Arquitectura Viva, Madrid, Spain

2021 *Kengo Kuma: Topography*, The Images Publishing Group, Melbourne, Australia

Kengo Kuma: My Life as an Architect in Tokyo, Thames & Hudson, London, United Kingdom

Kengo Kuma and Phillip Jodidio, *Kuma: Complete Works 1998–Today*, Taschen, Köln, Germany

KUMA Kengo: WOOD—Materiality of Architecture, Culture Convenience Club, Tokyo, Japan

2022 *Kengo Kuma: Zen Shigoto [The Complete Works]*, Daiwa Shobo, Tokyo, Japan

2023 *Nihon no Kenchiku [Architecture of Japan]*, Iwanami Shoten, Tokyo, Japan

Kengo Kuma: Arquitectura 1994–2022, Rural & Neo Rural, TC Cuadernos, Valencia, Spain

Luis Fernández-Galiano and Juhani Pallasmaa, *Kengo Kuma*, Arquitectura Viva, Madrid, Spain

Kengo Kuma: Arquitectura 2006–2024, Urban, TC Cuadernos, Valencia, Spain

2024 *Point Line Plane*, Thames & Hudson, London, United Kingdom

Kengo Kuma: Onomatopoeia Architecture Grounding, X-Knowledge, Tokyo, Japan

Published in Australia in 2025 by
The Images Publishing Group Pty Ltd
ABN 89 059 734 431

Offices

Melbourne
Waterman Business Centre
Suite 64, Level 2 UL40
1341 Dandenong Road
Chadstone, Victoria 3148
Australia
Tel: +61 3 8564 8122

New York
6 West 18th Street 4B
New York, NY 10011
United States
Tel: +1 212 645 1111

Shanghai
6F, Building C, 838 Guangji Road
Hongkou District, Shanghai 200434
China
Tel: +86 021 31260822

books@imagespublishing.com
www.imagespublishing.com

The Images Publishing Group Reference Number: IM1722

All drawings, renderings, and plans are supplied courtesy of the architect.

All photography is attributed in the project credits throughout the book, unless otherwise noted.
Front and back cover: Imagen Subliminal (Casa Batlló Stairs); page 6: Keishin Horikoshi and Kosuke Nakao / SS Tokyo (Nakahashi).

A catalogue record for this book is available from the National Library of Australia

Title: Kengo Kuma: Substance
Author: Kengo Kuma
ISBN: 9781864709926

This title was commissioned in IMAGES' Melbourne office and produced as follows:
Project Coordination Mariko Inaba, Kengo Kuma & Associates; *Creative Direction* Nicole Boehringer; *Editorial* Rebecca Gross, Jeanette Wall; *Production* Simon Walsh, Heather Johnson

EU GPSR Authorised Representative: Easy Access System Europe Oü
Company Registration ID: 16879218 | Address: Mustamäe tee 50, 10621 Tallinn, Estonia
Email: gpsr@easproject.com | Tel: +358 40 500 3575

Printed on 157gsm Chinese OJI matt art paper by Artron Art (Group) Co., Ltd, in China

IMAGES has included on its website a page for special notices in relation to this and its other publications.
Please visit www.imagespublishing.com